MORE IMAGES OF

SHEFFIELD

Happy 80th Birthday
Dennis
Love Karl + Graham
Hope you enjoy it.

The Star

MORE IMAGES OF

SHEFFIELD

First published in Great Britain by
The Breedon Books Publishing Company Limited
3 The Parker Centre, Mansfield Road, Derby, DE21 4SZ
1994, Softback edition 2004

ISBN 1 85983 445 0

Printed and bound by Scotprint, Haddington, Scotland.

Contents

Acknowledgements

We wish to thank the following for their help in compiling *More Images of Sheffield*:

Kendall Chambers, David H.A. (and Anthea) Nicol, Keith Hoyland and Worrall Male Voice Choir, Brenda Brierley, Nicola Ball, Bette Trenchard, Jacqui Unwin, Derek Brown and T.W.(Billy) Hoyland.

Also special thanks to Pauline Shearstone, the well-known Sheffield artist (her studios are in Ecclesall Road), for permission to reproduce several of her drawings.

We have included, too, pictures loaned to *The Star* by Raymond Hey and originally collected by Jim Bailey. (Anyone with a special interest in tram pictures should see *The Star's* special *Tram Tracks* supplement, published in April 1994).

We especially thank Keith Farnsworth, who, as in the first volume, has endeavoured to make use of his local knowledge in gathering this selection of pictures, and, as well as producing captions which add to our interest and appreciation, has contributed several enlightening special pieces on certain famous people and places. Mr Farnsworth is a well-known local author and journalist who worked for Sheffield Newspapers for many years and is now a freelance.

Foreword

I AM delighted that *The Star* has been able to bring to you a follow-up book to our successful *Images of Sheffield* published in October 1993. The popularity of the first book left us in no doubt that there is a passionate and widespread interest in the city's history.

Many found the book a veritable voyage of discovery, its pages unlocking doors to the lifestyles of previous generations.

Young and old alike found fascination in the way our ancestors worked and played as the city evolved to become one of the biggest in England.

More Images of Sheffield is a further attempt – and we believe a successful one – to satisfy that thirst for knowledge of the city's past. This time there is more emphasis on the suburbs, although the city centre is by no means neglected.

Sheffield's fine sporting tradition, too, is dramatically recaptured in words and pictures, with the stalwarts of a bygone age parading their skills to an admiring public. They didn't call them superstars then, but that is what they were.

As with *Images of Sheffield*, many of the pictures are drawn from our archives and they will stir memories and stimulate discussion.

We hope you enjoy this second book and that it serves as a permanent reminder of our rich heritage.

Peter Charlton
Editor
The Star
October 1994

More Images of Sheffield

This famous woodcut of Thomas Oughtibridge's north perspective of Sheffield in 1736 suggests a largely rural Sheffield in the era of water power some 50 years before Messrs Proctor established the first steam-driven grinding wheel in the town on the east side of the town. This was, however, a tough period for the local craftsmen, and some had been attracted by advertisements suggesting there were great advantages in emigrating to France. In the event, they didn't go, and stayed instead to fight against hard times and helped contribute to Sheffield's gradual industrial expansion through a succession of booms and slumps. Around 1747 Joseph Broadbent, the merchant, first established a foreign trade for local wares, and that marked the beginning of a new era.

Sheffield Manor House

A panoramic view of Sheffield, with Norfolk Park in the foreground. Looking across from the Midland Railway tracks, we can see that many of the old properties on Howard Street remain, and, top side of the Wedding cake-shaped Register office, the Town Hall extensions have yet to be started, while, to the right, we still have the old Pond Street bus station, the Joseph Rodgers buildings are still there, and the Sheaf Baths, which failed because they hadn't been built to Olympic standards, remain in operation. There's much more to spot …Isn't it fascinating looking at views like this?

This 1968 view of Sheffield from Hyde Park flats pre-dates the Park Square development. Looking down Broad Street, we see the foot of Duke Street, and, to the right, the Canal Wharf and other buildings which have disappeared. However, looking towards the skyline, we can spot some famous old buildings and some newer ones with which we are all now very familiar.

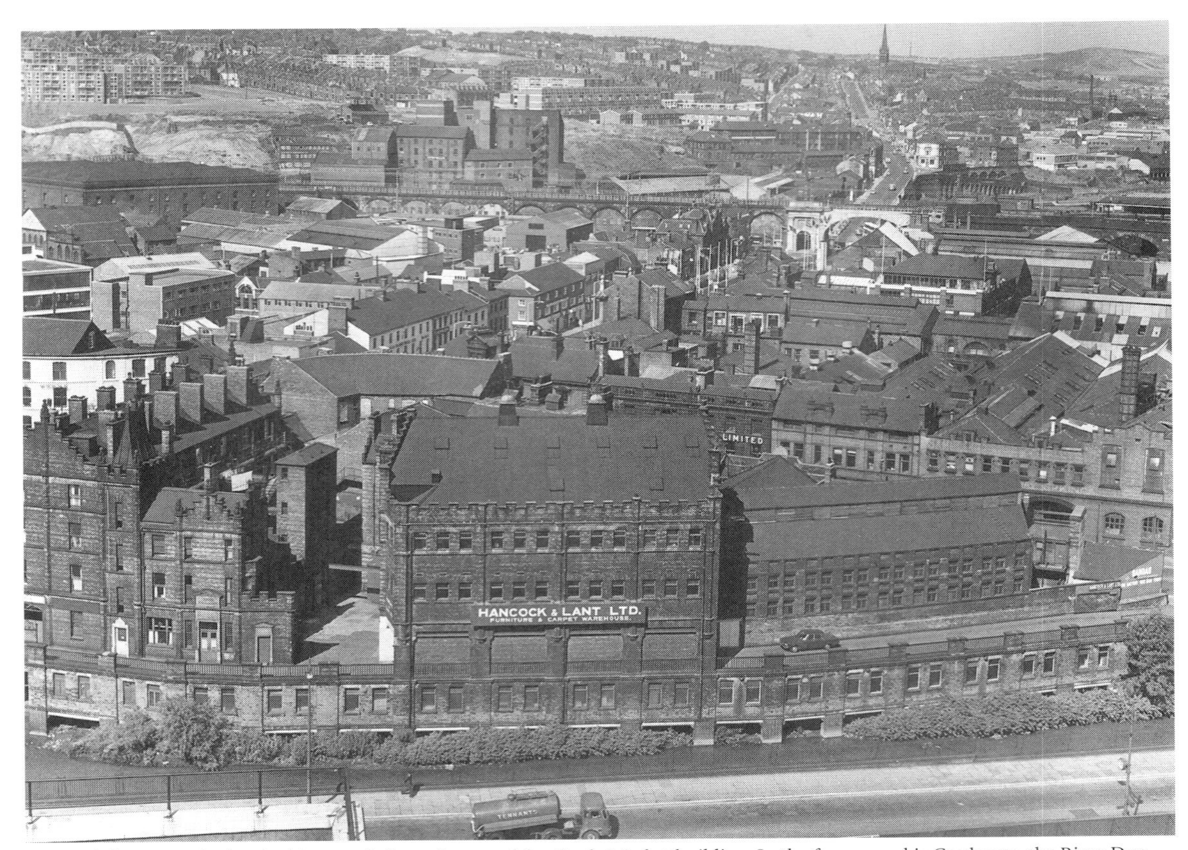

A splendid panoramic view looking north from the top of the Castle Market building. In the foreground is Castlegate, the River Don and the back of the buildings on this side of Blonk Street. We can see a lot of the Wicker Viaduct, with the Arches themselves standing out, and, beyond them, Spital Hill, the Albion pub which stood at what we now know as Caborn Corner (end of Carlisle Street), and the spire of All Saint's Church (John Brown built it).

Looking from above Upperthorpe towards Neepsend and the gasholder which overshadowed houses in old Farfield Road (if you went in one, it always seemed dark!), plus the towers of the power station. And there's plenty more landmarks to pick out.

Central Sheffield

A view looking down Church Street towards High Street. Note Hartley Seed's old bookshop on the left, part of a row of properties which have long since disappeared, although the buildings further down have survived.

A Sheffield Fire Service parade in the 1960s, the band marching up Church Street, about to enter Leopold Street.

Men in bowler hats stand in groups in Church Street discussing events at the meeting they have just left in the Cutlers Hall. Several other men, in cloth caps, seem to be wondering whether this gathering of employers might mean work for them, this being that phase between the wars when many were on the dole.

Sheffield Cathedral about 100 years ago.

The old Blue Coat School, where railings were fixed on the roof to enable pupils to use it as a playground – a step taken after the authorities at the Cathedral had complained the boys should not be playing in their grounds!

The bottom of Church Street in 1867, with Cole Brothers store on the corner of Fargate. This was about the time the Cutler's Hall was being substantially extended.

Old Campo Lane before it was widened.

Another view of old Campo Lane.

Hartshead, and the corner of Aldine Court, will ever be linked with the office of James Montgomery's *Iris*, a famous local newspaper in the early years of the 19th century – when it was not always profitable to be an editor.

THERE IS A CALM FOR THOSE THAT WEEP,
A REST FOR WEARY PILGRIMS FOUND,
THEY SOFTLY LIE AND SWEETLY SLEEP,
LOW ON THE GROUND.
THE STORM THAT WRECKS THE WINTRY SKY,
NO MORE DISTURBS THEIR DEEP REPOSE,
THAN SUMMER EVENINGS LATEST SIGH
THAT SHUTS THE ROSE.
THE SOUL OF ORIGIN DIVINE,
GODS GLORIOUS IMAGE FREED FROM CLAY,
LEEDS & HOLBECK
LEEDS & HOLBECK BUIL

Perhaps it is appropriate that the statue of James Montgomery now stands in the shadow of Sheffield Cathedral, a stone throw from Hartshead, being removed there after spending years in the old Sheffield Cemetery, where it was forgotten and seldom seen. This picture shows the Bishop of Sheffield rededicating the statue of the famous poet, hymn writer and journalist at a ceremony in June 1971.

The Iris;
OR, THE SHEFFIELD ADVERTISER.

"[illegible] AND THE PLACE OF FAIR DELIGHTFUL PEACE, [illegible] BY PARTY RAGE TO LIVE LIKE BROTHERS."

PRINTED AND PUBLISHED BY JAMES MONTGOMERY, HARTSHEAD.

No. 1915.—Vol. XXXVI. TUESDAY, FEBRUARY 17, 1824. Price Sevenpence.

THE PICTURE OF SHEFFIELD.

THIS DAY is published, in a neat Pocket Volume, price [illegible], THE PICTURE OF SHEFFIELD; or, an Historical and Descriptive View of the Town of Sheffield, in the county of York, to which is prefixed a ... description of the Township of [illegible] ... with a PLAN of the TOWN; also the following Wood Engravings, neatly executed:—

View of the Parish Church.
—— St. George's Church.
—— [illegible] Chapel.
—— the New Grammar School.
—— the Music Hall.
—— the Infirmary.
—— Christ's Church, Attercliffe.

A few Copies are printed on large Paper, with Plates on India Paper, price [illegible].

Sheffield: Printed and published by Gorman Ridge, [illegible].

ASSOCIATION FOR THE PROSECUTION OF FELONS, &c.

THE ANNUAL MEETING of the Association for the Prosecution of Felons, will be held at the House of Mr. [illegible], the George Inn, on Friday, the 20th [illegible] ... for the purpose of receiving the Report of the Proceedings of the past Year, collecting the Annual Subscriptions, and transacting the General Business of the Association, &c.

The Committee intend to dine together on Thursday, the 26th [illegible], and they respectfully solicit the company of as many of the Members as can make it convenient to attend.

Dinner on the Table precisely at Three o'Clock.

By Order, E. WOOD, Secretary.

Feb. 12, 1824.

LEEDS, BRADFORD, & OWLERTON CHAPELS.

Notice is hereby given,

TO all Persons who are desirous of delivering Estimates or Tenders for Building the above Chapels, that the Specifications, Plans, and Working Drawings for the same ... may be seen at my Office, in [illegible], Sheffield, on Monday, the 9th of February, where they will remain till the 24th of the same month.

Every Tender must be delivered at my Office, sealed up, signed by the parties, with the names of two responsible Persons as Sureties, on or before the 1st day of March.

JOS. BOTHAM, Architect.

Feb. 2, 1824.

NOTICE IS HEREBY GIVEN,

THAT the Partnership formerly subsisting between the undersigned FRANCIS CASTLETON, JAMES MILNER, and GEORGE PARKIN, in the trade of a [illegible], carried on at Sheffield, in the county of York, under the Firm of "Castleton, Milner, & Parkin," was dissolved on the Twenty-second day of January, one thousand eight hundred and twenty-two. Dated this [illegible] day of February, 1824.

FRANCIS CASTLETON,
JAMES MILNER,
GEORGE PARKIN.

Witness, [illegible].

BENJAMIN PLANT'S ASSIGNMENT.

BENJAMIN PLANT, of Little Sheffield, in the parish of Sheffield, in the county of York, [illegible], hath by Indenture, bearing Date the [illegible] ... assigned all his Estate and Effects, to Trustees, for the equal benefit of all his Creditors ... Two Months from the date thereof.

NOTICE IS HEREBY GIVEN,

[illegible] ... Deed of Assignment lies for Signature at the Office of Mr. Rodgers, Solicitor, Sheffield; and such of the Creditors as neglect to execute the same within the [illegible] ... will be excluded from the Benefit of the Dividend intended to be made immediately afterwards.

ROBERT RODGERS, Solicitor.

Sheffield, 10th February, 1824.

FREEHOLD HOMESTEAD AND [illegible] LANDS, AT DORE AND TOTLEY.

TO BE SOLD BY PRIVATE CONTRACT,

A VERY [illegible] FREEHOLD ESTATE, consisting of a substantial and convenient Homestead, and several Closes and Parcels of Land, situate at Dore, in the parish of Dronfield, in the county of Derby, containing together [illegible], and now in the possession of Mr. John Unwin.

Also, TWO CLOSES of excellent LAND, situate at Totley, in the parish of Dronfield aforesaid, containing 6a. 0r. 4p. now in the occupation of George Dalton.

A considerable portion of the Land at Dore contains valuable Beds of Coal, which may be easily gotten, and would find a ready sale.

The Premises will be divided into Lots to suit Purchasers, and part of the Purchase Money may remain on security.

For all further particulars, and to treat for the Purchase, application may be made to Mr. John Unwin, of Dore, the Owner, or to Mr. BROOKFIELD, Solicitor, Sheffield.

Sheffield, 12th Feb. 1824.

DR. STEER'S OPODELDOC

IS superior to all other external applications for the cure of Sprains, Bruises, Rheumatism, Cramp, Chilblains, &c. For Chilblains it should be dissolved and applied on their first appearance, to prevent their breaking. Spurious imitations of this excellent Remedy, by persons who even make use of Dr. Steer's name, are in circulation throughout the country; Purchasers must therefore be very particular in asking for Dr. Steer's Opodeldoc, prepared by F. Newbery & Sons, and carefully to observe the name "F. Newbery" engraved in the Stamp on each Bottle. Price 2s. 9d.

Sold by F. NEWBERY & SONS, at the original Warehouse for Dr. James's Powder, 45, St. Paul's, London; and, by their appointment, by Miss Gales, Sheffield; and by Agents in most country towns.

CHILBLAINS.

MARSHALL'S UNIVERSAL CERATE has maintained its reputation for nearly Forty Years past, and is still with confidence recommended for the prevention and cure of those troublesome and painful visitants Chilblains, whether in a broken or unbroken state; it removes the itching and inflammation on the first application, and when broken, heals in a much shorter time than can be credited but by experience.

Wounds, Ulcerated Legs, Burns, Scalds, Scorbutic Humours, Sore Nipples, Eruptions and Pimples in the Face, Breakings-out about the Mouth and Nose, Ringworms and Shingles, and Eruptions of every denomination, and however long standing, are effectually cured by this Cerate. Price 1s. 1½d. and 2s. 9d. per box.

Sold by Mrs. Marshall's Agent, E. EDWARDS, 67, St. Paul's Church-Yard, London; Miss Gales, Sheffield; and also by all the Booksellers and Druggists in Sheffield and the neighbouring towns.

To Steel-Converters & Refiners.

WANTED,

A MAN, to superintend either or both of the above Businesses. None need apply but Men of sober habits, and who perfectly understand their Trade.

For Particulars apply to MATTHIAS SPENCER and Son, [illegible], Sheffield.

SALES BY MR. SAUNDERS.

BANKRUPTS' EFFECTS,
Free from Auction Duty.

Tools, Materials, Fixtures, remaining Stock of White Metal Goods, Glass Cases, a Patent double-power six horse Steam-engine complete, Shafts, Drums, Bands, a pair of Metal Rollers, Stamp, &c. &c.

TO BE SOLD BY AUCTION,
(Without Reserve,)
By Mr. SAUNDERS,

By order of the Assignees of Messrs. Green, Sampson, and Smith, on Wednesday, the 18th day of February, 1824, at the Warehouse and Workshops of the said Messrs. Green, Sampson, & Smith, in Sheffield Park;

ALL THE

REMAINING stock-in-trade, tools, materials, fixtures, and other effects, on the premises, comprehending metal tea and coffee pots, sugar basins, cream jugs, ink stands, pepper boxes, mustards, [illegible], tureens, hash dishes, and other finished stock, also a quantity of brown, white, and tissue paper, a quantity of leather and skins, nearly 4 cwts. of spelter, a large quantity of lead and Britannia metal, teapot knobs and handles, [illegible], metal weights and Truss ways, a large draw bench, in excellent condition, with spindles and whirlies complete; a very good stamp with the appendages complete, a quantity of [illegible], workboards, slides and leather drins, stocks, boxes, drawers, shelves, ingot and other moulds, a metal stove with drying boards complete, a wheelbarrow, wood [illegible], melting pots and frames, ranges, a very good glass show case, warehouse tables, a large counting house desk with drawers, and various other tools, materials, and fixtures.

Likewise will be Sold by Auction, in a short time (time and place to be specified in a future advertisement,) an excellent six-horse double power Steam-engine, with boiler, eight horse cylinder, &c. complete, and in good working order, having been manufactured by Messrs. Peel and Williams, of Manchester, in the year 1820, and considered at least equal to any engine in this neighbourhood of the same power; drums, bands, and other machinery connected therewith, and likewise an excellent pair of large metal rollers, with housings, &c. complete, sold [illegible] by Messrs. Dodge.

The Auction will commence at Ten o'clock each [illegible].

VERY ELEGANT

HOUSEHOLD FURNITURE,

Stock of Glass-Cases and Straps, Cabinet-Cases, Paper, Leather, Materials, Tools, and Fixtures; Exempt from Auction Duty.

TO BE SOLD BY AUCTION,
BY MR. SAUNDERS,
(Without Reserve,)

On Thursday and Friday next, the 19th and 20th days of February, 1824, at the House and Warehouse of Mr. Samuel [illegible], in [illegible], Sheffield,

ALL THE

ELEGANT HOUSEHOLD FURNITURE,
Stock, Tools, Materials, Fixtures, and other Effects on the Premises.

THE FURNITURE comprises an elegant four-post mahogany bedstead, with fluted and massive pillars, dome top, and cornice and [illegible], bottom richly hung with dove-coloured moreen, tastefully decorated, and window curtains to match; [illegible] mahogany bedstead, fully hung with chintz furniture, and window curtains to match; a camp bedstead, hung with dimity; three excellent [illegible] feather-beds, with extra large bolsters and pillows, [illegible] and superior bedding, a very good solid mahogany [illegible], with [illegible] slides, swing-glasses, Venetian and superfine Scotch bed and stair carpeting, bedsteps, [illegible] chairs, with [illegible], sofa and [illegible], with square and [illegible] washstands, a set of very elegant [illegible] chairs, in beautiful condition, with 2 elbow do., 2 [illegible] hair Grecian sofa, [illegible] and loose cushions; a very [illegible] set of [illegible] on pillars, a large pier glass, in gilt frame, with excellent plate, two superfine Brussels hearth carpets, a mahogany [illegible] and bookcase, brass fenders and polished fire-irons, [illegible], plate, books, china, glass, a valuable model of His Majesty, four interesting engravings framed, plated [illegible], [illegible] and other chairs and tables, [illegible] of dove-coloured moreen window hangings, expensively trimmed, with elegant poles and pins, two sets of chintz do., an eight days' clock, a complete assortment of [illegible], [illegible] and culinary utensils, glass bottles, earthenware, a good kitchen dresser, with cupboards, and all other useful articles of furniture.

The STOCK IN TRADE, Materials, Tools, and Fixtures, consist of a quantity of leather of various kinds, tissue and brown paper, razors, cases, and straps, finished, and some in the various stages of manufacture, patterns, tables, workboards, desks, cupboard, partition and door, large show case, with glass slides, cutting-boards, and various other matters.

The Furniture is uncommonly good, both in respect of material and workmanship, and is in [illegible] beautiful condition.

The Auction will commence at Ten o'clock each day.

The Furniture will be Sold the First day, and the Stock &c. on the Second.

CAPITAL FREEHOLD

DWELLING-HOUSE, OFFICES, &c. &c.

TO BE SOLD BY AUCTION,
BY Mr. W. H. SAUNDERS,

At the Auction Mart, East Parade, Sheffield, on Tuesday, the 9th day of March next, at Six o'clock in the Evening, subject to such Conditions as will be then produced;

ALL that excellent MESSUAGE or DWELLING-HOUSE, with the Stable, Outbuildings, and Appurtenances thereto belonging, situate at the corner of Norfolk-row, and also fronting to Norfolk-street, in Sheffield aforesaid, as the same are now in the possession of Mrs. Wilkinson. And also all those very convenient and pleasantly situated OFFICES adjoining the said Dwelling-house, now in the possession of Mr. Frederick Wilkinson, Solicitor, but who is changing his residence.

The above Property is most substantially built and well finished, is in excellent repair, and is one of the best situations in the town for an Attorney, or a Medical Man, and has the advantage of an abundant supply of both hard and soft Water.

A Purchaser may be accommodated with one half of the purchase money on security of the Premises.

For further Particulars, and for a view, apply to Mr. Wilkinson, (the Owner,) at his Offices, in Norfolk-row.

Sheffield, Feb. 13, 1824.

WILL OPEN FOR EXHIBITION,
IN THE THEATRE,
On Tuesday, the 17th Inst., for a short time only,
BARKER & Co.'s
GRAND
PERISTREPHIC PANORAMAS
(FIRST SERIES)
Of the DEFEAT of the TURKS
AT
[illegible]

View 1.—The City of Jerusalem, the capital of [illegible].

View 2.—The Lake Latakieh, with [illegible].

View 3.—The Defeat of the Turks by the Greeks; Men, Women, and Children are seen engaged in the Defence of their Country.

View 4.—The Interior of the Council Chamber, as it appeared when the Governor was killed, whilst surrounded by Officers, and deserted by the Ministers of the Porte.

View 5.—The Battles of Ligny and Waterloo.

View 6.—The Flight of Buonaparte, and Retreat of the French Army from the Field.

View 7.—The taking of Buonaparte's Carriage, and the battle of Genappe.

View 8.—The Village of Waterloo, as it appeared the morning after the Battle, with wounded Officers and Men; 10,000 Figures size of life, painted from Drawings taken on the spot, on 10,000 square feet of canvas.

The movements are accompanied by a Military Band, and a correct description given of each View.

There will be an Exhibition each day at Twelve and at Two o'clock; and to accommodate Families from the Country, there will be an extra Exhibition every Tuesday and Saturday, at Three o'clock.

In the Evenings, the Panorama will be brilliantly Illuminated, and exhibited at Seven o'clock; the last exhibition precisely at half-past Eight.

Admission, Boxes, 2s.—Gallery, 1s.—Children, Half Price.—Season Tickets, Boxes, 7s. 6d.—Gallery, 5s.

The Views given of the Battle of Waterloo will be found different to any thing before exhibited in this town under that name.

For particulars, see books and bills. Constant Fires are kept in the Theatre.

WOOD SALE.

TO BE SOLD BY TICKET,

At the Rose and Crown-Inn, in Penistone, on Thursday, Feb. 26, 1824, at Three o'clock in the Afternoon, subject to Conditions;

IN Bay Croft Wood, in Denby, and in Holt and Hedge Rows in Samuel Shaw and Joseph Gaunt's Farms.

565 Trees, numbered with scribe-irons.
478 Oak Poles, scratched with do.
311 Ash do.
1 Beech do.
167 Birch do. and Alder.

At the Green, near Midhope, in Half Hall Wood, the Rough and Hedge Rows in John Hallifield's Farm.

180 Trees, numbered.
144 Oak Poles, scratched.
8 Ash do.
5 Sycamore do.
4 Crab.
968 Birch and Alder.

Coats Woods, near Silkstone, and Cow Fall Wood,

196 Trees, numbered with scribe-irons.
280 Oak Poles, scratched.
95 Ash do.
177 Birch and Alder.

Stubbing Wood, with the Low Part,

575 Trees, numbered.
478 Oak Poles.
38 Ash.
14 Elm.
6 Beech.
5 Crab.
180 Birch do.

North Royd's Wood,

215 Trees, numbered.
304 Oak Poles.
85 Ash.
6 Elm.
80 Birch and Alder.
With the Hedge-Rows in the Farms.

Also, at the Wire-Mills, in Thurgoland, in Wire-Mill Holme,

44 Trees, numbered.
14 Alder Poles.

To view the Bay Croft Wood and Hedge-Rows, apply to James Haliwell, Nether Denby; to view the Wood at the Green, apply to John Hallifield, at the Green; and the Wood at Coats, to Adam Batty, Lower Coats; and to Joseph Cauldwell, of [illegible], for the Wood at the Wire Mills.

ALSO TO BE SOLD,

At Wm. Brighton's, the Angel-inn, at Ryon's Green, on Friday, 27th Inst.

In Fox Field Spring, near Chapeltown,

129 Trees, numbered with scribe-irons.
390 Oak Poles, scratched.
55 Ash do.
1 Cherry do.
2 Birch do.
16 Sycamore.

For further particulars, apply to Mr. Wm. Smith, Solicitor, Bank-street, Sheffield; or to Mr. James Oates, of Greenside.

PEARSON'S BANKRUPTCY.

WHEREAS a Commission of Bankrupt is awarded and issued forth against THOMAS PEARSON, now or late of [illegible], in the parish of Whiston, in the county of York, miller, dealer and chapman, and he being declared a Bankrupt, is hereby required to surrender himself to the Commissioners in the said Commission named, or the major part of them, on the Twenty-fifth and Twenty-sixth Days of February instant, and on the Twentieth Day of March next, at Eleven in the Forenoon on each of the said days, at the College Inn, in Rotherham, in the said county, and make a full discovery and disclosure of his Estate and Effects; when and where the Creditors are to come prepared to prove their Debts; and at the second sitting to chuse Assignees; and at the last sitting the said Bankrupt is required to finish his examination, and the Creditors are to assent to or dissent from the allowance of his Certificate.—All Persons indebted to the said Bankrupt, or that have any of his Effects, are not to pay or deliver the same but to whom the Commissioners shall appoint, but to give notice to Messrs. Wigglesworth and Ridsdale, solicitors, Gray's Inn, London, or to Mr. Nicholson, solicitor, Wath-upon-Dearne, near Rotherham.

WANTED,

A TILTER, who well understands his business. Apply to Messrs. NAYLOR and SANDERSON, [illegible].

Sheffield, Feb. 14, 1824.

ARCHITECTURAL LIBRARY, 59, HIGH HOLBORN.

This Day is published, the Second Edition, improved and enlarged, illustrated with Four Plates and several Wood Cuts, Price 12s. Boards,

PRACTICAL ESSAY on the STRENGTH of CAST IRON, and OTHER METALS; intended for the Assistance of Engineers, Iron-Masters, Architects, Millwrights, Founders, and others engaged in the Construction of Machines, Buildings, &c.; containing Practical Rules, Tables, and Examples ... Tables of the Properties of Materials.

By THOMAS TREDGOLD,

Civil Engineer, Member of the Institution of Civil Engineers, Author of Elementary Principles of Carpentry, &c. &c.

Printed for J. TAYLOR, at the Architectural Library, No. 59, High Holborn.

Shortly will be published, by the same Author, PRINCIPLES of WARMING and VENTILATING PUBLIC BUILDINGS, MANUFACTORIES, HOSPITALS, &c.; with Remarks on the Nature of Heat, &c. With Plates.

PRACTICAL MECHANICS.

Just published, handsomely printed in 2 vols. 8vo. Illustrated with 20 Plates and numerous Figures, Price £1 6s. bds.

PRACTICAL ESSAYS on MILL WORK and other MACHINERY; viz. on the Teeth of Wheels; the Shafts, Gudgeons, and Journals of Machines; the Couplings and Bearings of Shafts; Disengaging and Re-engaging Machinery in Motion; Equalizing the Motion of Mills; Changing the Velocity of Machines in Motion; and the Framing of Mill-Work, with several useful Tables. By Robertson Buchanan, Engineer. The Second Edition, revised, with Notes and additional Articles, containing new Researches on various Mechanical Subjects. By Thomas Tredgold, Civil Engineer, &c.

Printed for J. TAYLOR, at the Architectural Library, 59, High Holborn.

Also, handsomely printed in Octavo, illustrated with Two large Plates, Price 6s. sewed,

DESCRIPTION of a RAIL-WAY, on a new Principle; with Observations on those hitherto constructed, and a Table showing the comparative Amount of Resistance on several now in Use; and a Description of an Improved Dynamometer, for ascertaining the Resistance of floating Vessels, and Carriages moving on Roads and Railways. By H. R. Palmer, Civil Engineer.

Where also may be had,

SMEATON's REPORTS on CIVIL ENGINEERING. Seventy-three Plates. 4 vols. 4to. £8 10s. Boards.

For INDIGESTION, JAUNDICE, LOSS of APPETITE, and other DISORDERS dependent on a deranged State of the LIVER, and of the BILIARY and DIGESTIVE ORGANS,

SMITH'S Genuine LEAMINGTON SALTS are confidently offered to the public under the recommendation of Dr. Kerr, Northampton; Dr. Thackeray, Chester; Dr. Wake, Warwick; Dr. Middleton, Leamington; Dr. Thackeray, Cambridge; Dr. Lomax, Warwick; Dr. Weatherhead, Henley, Oxon.

The peculiar Efficacy of the Leamington Waters in the Cure of the above-named and many other Disorders, having been so generally acknowledged, renders it almost unnecessary (especially when offered under such recommendation) to address any thing in favour of these Salts; except that they have been satisfactorily proved, both by chemical analysis and medical experience, to possess all the Tonic, Aperient, and other active Properties of the Waters: so that those persons who have been hitherto prevented, by distance or other causes, from availing themselves of the Curative Powers of those celebrated Springs, may now be supplied with a substitute, possessing all their beneficial qualities. These Salts are prepared by evaporating to dryness the Waters at the Original Baths Leamington.

Sold in Bottles, price 2s. 9d. and 4s. 6d. each, Duty included; Wholesale and Retail, by Mr. Smith, the Proprietor, at his Pump-Room; Mr. Genever, at the Depot, Bath-street, Leamington; and Messrs. Barclay and Sons, Fleet-Market, London.

☞ Ask for Smith's LEAMINGTON SALTS.

Sold retail by

Gales, Todd, Ridge, James, Green, Whitaker, Taylor, Loader, and Harrison, Sheffield; Wilson, Crookes, and Norton, Rotherham; Best, and Cooper, Barnsley; Wright, Doncaster; Collinson, Bawtry, Thorne, Drury, Mansfield; Ford, Hunstead, and Butler, Chesterfield; Siddall, and Walters, Alfreton; Greasley, Retford; Reinhardt, Nichols, [illegible], and Lawton, Wakefield; also by the principal Druggists, Booksellers, and Medicine Venders in every Town throughout the United Kingdom.

WELL WORTHY THE ATTENTION OF PARENTS.

Macclesfield, January [illegible], 1824.

GENTLEMEN,—Believe me, it is with the most heartfelt gratitude I communicate, for publication, the following facts:—About twelve months ago, my daughter Charlotte became afflicted with a very virulent Scorbutic Complaint. It commenced when she was six years old, with a scaly eruption on her leg; this was at first neglected, but in four months, it having increased to such a degree as nearly to cover the whole of her body, we became alarmed, and used a great variety both of internal and external applications, without deriving the least benefit. The great celebrity your Antiscorbutic Drops have attained in this neighbourhood, and the recommendation of a friend, who had experienced their beneficial effects, induced me to give them a trial, and I assure you I had no reason to repent it, for before she had taken them long, an evident improvement took place, and in three months the cure was completed. I purchased your Drops from Mr. Richard Wright, Chemist, &c. 112, Mill-street, and as he saw my daughter both before and after her recovery, any enquiries will get further particulars on application to him, or to, Gentlemen, your obedient and grateful servant,

GEORGE WHITTAKER,
Cabinet Maker, &c., Macclesfield, Macclesfield.

Attested by Mr. Richard Wright, Chemist, &c., 112, Mill-street.

To Messrs. John Lignum & Son, Surgeons, Manchester.

These Drops are sold in moulded square bottles, at 2s. 9d., 4s. 6d., and 11s. (one 11s. bottle is equal to three 4s. 6d. and six 2s. 9d. ones), by John Lignum & Son, No. [illegible], Bridge-street, Manchester, and by Miss Gales, Wm. Todd, G. Ridge, T. Orton, booksellers, and J. James, druggist, Sheffield; M. Wilson, bookseller, Rotherham; W. Sheardown & Son, do., Doncaster; John Ford, do., Chesterfield; John Fox, do., Pontefract; R. Nichols, do., Wakefield; T. England, druggist, Huddersfield; and by one or more respectable medicine-venders in every market-town in the united kingdom.—Of whom also may be had, Mr. Lignum's IMPROVED LOTION, for all Scorbutic Eruptions, [illegible] duty included.

Markets.

CORN EXCHANGE, LONDON.
Feb. 16, 1824.

[illegible]

CURRENT PRICES OF GRAIN.

[illegible]

WAKEFIELD CORN MARKET, Feb. 16.

[illegible]

AVERAGE PRICES OF CORN.
In England and Wales, taken from the Gazette.

[illegible]

PRICE OF HOPS.

[illegible]

PRICES OF TALLOW.

[illegible]

PRICE OF LEATHER IN LONDON.

[illegible]

RAW HIDES, ⅌ stone of 8 lbs.

[illegible]

Bankrupts.

LONDON GAZETTE, FEB. 14.

[illegible]

DIVIDENDS.

[illegible]

CERTIFICATES.—MAR. 6.

[illegible]

PARTNERSHIP DISSOLVED.

F. Castleton, J. Milner, and G. Parkin, Sheffield, [illegible].

SCOTCH BANKRUPT.

G. M'GILL, [illegible].

The *Sheffield Iris*, which has a special place in local newspaper history.

Looking up from Hartshead, beyond Banker's House to the right, and into Campo Lane.

The old Dove & Rainbow pub, in Hartshead, where many a Sheffield journalist found inspiration, or told tall tales about stories that got away!

From Paradise Square to Page Hall – The Tale of Thomas Broadbent

IT is true that there is a story everywhere you look. A classic example is how the old Banker's House in Hartshead, and Page Hall, near Firth Park, evoke the saga of an ambitious Sheffielder called Thomas Broadbent and his family's long-running feud with the Roebucks.

Banker's House, the front of which looks up York Street, was built in 1728 by Broadbent's grandfather, Nicholas, and it was here in 1774 that young Thomas founded one of the earliest private banks in the town.

All went so well that Thomas was inspired to embark on the building of a mansion he called Page Hall. Then, in 1780, his bank suddenly failed ...and, with his fine new home still unfinished, he had little choice but to mortgage the property to help meet his debts.

Page Hall later passed in the hands of James Dixon, head of the famous silver plating works in Cornish Place, and the estate was acquired by Mark Firth in 1874, when the legendary steelmaster immediately donated all except about three of the 39 acres to the town for the creation of Firth Park. The building survives, obscured from view by the houses on Firth Park Road, but it is a shadow of the place it once was, and it is difficult to recognise that, when it was built, it was a home on a scale previously unknown in the town.

It has not survived as well as Banker's House, a property still serving the cause of commerce in the later years of the 20th century. This property first passed to the Turner family, then to the Binneys, later being occupied by a succession of lawyers as it graduated into a building synonymous with use as offices.

The Broadbents were also involved in the creation of Paradise Square ...and explain why it was so named.

Paradise Square was once known as the place where some of the great meetings and gatherings were held in the old town, and many legendary figures addressed the multitudes from the famous old steps. Yet it had been a cornfield with the name Hick Stile Field until about 1736, when local merchant Joseph Broadbent built five houses along one end of the area.

For some reason, he gave them the name Paradise Row. Then, in 1771, his son, banker-to-be Thomas, obtained a lease on the cornfield and offered it for sub-lease as building lots. Thus a square of buildings was created, and it took the same name as the original row of houses.

Moreover, Paradise was also seized upon by businessmen occupying properties in what was then Workhouse Lane (because it had led to the workhouse) and they decided Paradise Street was a much more appropriate address!

The rise and fall of Thomas Broadbent was like something out an epic historical novel, and the rivalry between his family and the Roebucks went back 20 or more years before he founded his bank.

In 1753 his father, Joseph, had been a popular choice as candidate for election as a Town Trustee, but Ben Roebuck, who held the post of Town Collector, insisted on nominating Thomas Newbould in direct opposition to Broadbent. In the event, Broadbent enjoyed an overwhelming victory, but mutual ill-feeling remained.

The irony was that the Broadbents and the Roebucks had led the way in terms of commercial enterprise which had opened up foreign markets to Sheffield companies for the first time. Then, when the Roebucks emerged as leaders in banking, too, the Broadbents were quick to show they could also succeed in this field.

There was great jubilation in the Broadbent family when, in 1778, the Roebuck's banking enterprise failed, but their joy was short-lived because of the collapse of Thomas's bank two years later. Ben Roebuck had to give up the mansion he had built at Meersbrook, now Broadbent had to relinquish Page Hall. Both men had been regarded as candidates for a mighty fall because of their ambition and the flamboyance with which they had splashed their money on expensive and luxurious homes.

Few people shed tears for either man, but the great frustration for Broadbent was that Roebuck emerged with the greater public sympathy. Both families reverted to the business of merchanting, but, by the end of the 18th century, two of the most famous early commercial names had disappeared from the town ...and the only reminders of their fame are the properties and places which, by virtue of their history. will always have a story to tell. Roebuck's Meersbrook property, which stands in Meersbrook Park, became the Ruskin Museum.

Banker's House.

Page Hall.

Paradise Square.

Meersbrook House (Ruskin Museum).

W.C.Leng – The Man Who Exposed the Sheffield Outrages

Sir William C.Leng (1825-1902) has passed into the folklore of Sheffield journalism as a legendary campaigning editor, his name ever synonymous with the 19th century trades union outrages and his exposure of William Broadhead, secretary of the Saw Grinders' Union, as the man behind a series of attacks on non-union workmen which included one shooting and many attempts to blow up workshops and houses.

Leng, who arrived in the town in 1863 to become joint proprietor of the *Sheffield Telegraph*, got his first big chance to show his journalistic prowess with the Sheffield Flood of 1864,. but it was his fearless pursuit of the perpetrators of the local outrages, and his campaign for a Government Commission of Inquiry, which brought him fame.

Had he not been a newcomer (he was from Hull) he might never have tackled a problem which had existed for years, and, indeed, was accepted with a shrug by local people who viewed the situation as just the way of the Sheffield trades.

The Hereford Street outrage, in which gunpowder had been put down the cellar grate of the home of a grinder, causing an explosion which shattered the property, was the incident which prompted Leng to launch his campaign and pursue it in the face of threats on his life. He had the support of Chief Constable John Jackson, and the constant protection of the police. At the height of his exposures, he was often seen returning to his office, casually smoking his cigar while walking towards Aldine Court between two burly constables. Moreover, he kept a loaded revolver on his desk!

Leng's efforts led to the setting up of the Commission in 1867, when a parade of witnesses revealed a long catalogue of outrages and the men behind them. The Wild West had little on Sheffield in those days!

The story was touched upon and dealt with best in the original version of *The Stirrings in Sheffield*, initially produced at the old Playhouse in 1966 and revived at the Crucible. A more recent production, perhaps because it attempted to emphasise humour rather than drama, somehow failed to capture the true essence of a remarkable episode in local industrial history.

Left: William Broadhead.

Cover of programme for original Playhouse production of musical play based on the Outrages.

Before steam, power for grinding came from water wheels.

The Globe Works: the premises endured several famous outrages, mainly in the 1840s.

The late Billy Hukin was a modern razor grinder whose career was never dogged by the kind of industrial violence common in the 19th century.

The Black Swan in Pond Street before the first redevelopment of the area.

Looking down Pond Street as it is in the mid-1930s, it is difficult to imagine that it once looked like this, long before the creation of the bus station and the Sheffield City Polytechnic (later Hallam University).

For many people, the old Pond Street bus station was synonymous with going on holiday, for the bottom areas were reserved for coaches, some linked with the old Sheffield United Tours offices on the site. This picture was taken at the start of the big Sheffield Holiday Weeks in July 1958, and will be of great interest, not so much for readers hoping to spot someone they know as for viewing all those buildings in the distance which have long since gone.

A more recent shot of Pond Street, the old bus station, the former SUT building and part of what was once Joseph Rodgers' cutlery works but became offices of the Housing Department for a time. Park Hill flats and Hyde Park on the hillside. So much that can be seen in this picture has gone.

Fitzalan Square

There was a time when Fitzalan Square was probably as popular as Cole's Corner as a meeting place, for here was a tram terminus, a taxi rank and three landmarks (the GPO building, Marples pub, and the solid-looking Barclay's Bank) which you could hardly miss if someone nominated them as a place to rendezvous.

Moreover, there were two cinemas, the News Theatre and, from 1956 to 1971, the Odeon, and somewhere to shelter, if required, in the entrance to the White Building. There were also underground toilets in the heart of the Square, and, if you wanted to know where and when to catch a bus or tram, the Transport Department had offices a few steps from the King Edward VII statue.

In the early 1980s, the Square's centenary passed unmarked, perhaps because, at the time, it had fallen into neglect. That, of course, was the decade when fire gutted both the News Theatre and the nearby Wigfall's furniture and electrical store, and the last pint was served in the Bell Inn.

Yet Fitzalan Square, at the bottom of High Street, continues to evoke nostalgia: never quite fulfilling the role it was intended to fill, yet having an eventful enough career to claim an affectionate place in the memory of those who have known it well.

There aren't many people now who know that there was a time when Norfolk Street continued through to Bakers' Hill, or when Commercial Street ran along what is now the bottom side of the Square. More will recall that, until 1930, the old Fitzalan Market looked into the Square, and the old Marples' pub (the present one was completed in 1959) was hit in the Blitz of December 1940, with so many Christmas revellers buried in the debris.

The Fitzalan Square with which most of us have been familiar in modern times probably dates back to the 1909 improvement scheme which, at a cost of £9,00, saw the central area levelled and paved, and the erection of the oval stone balustraded terrace above the then-new underground toilets.

It was a year before this that the White Building was completed, its tiled frontage bearing etchings of ten Sheffield craftsmen, while, at the same time, the old Queen's Cutlery Works were sold and the splendid new General Post Office, built at a cost of £60,000, emerged in time for a formal opening in July 1910. It was then that the old Wonderland site was acquired for the creation of the Electra Palace, opened in February 1911 and boasting the novelty of a continuous film show between 3 and 10.30 pm daily. Its slogan was "Come when you please, leave when you please", with the show having a two-hour cycle.

The Square then needed a statue to give it the final touch, and King Edward VII (who had died in 1910) was the subject of the memorial unveiled in October 1913.

The Electra introduced sound in 1930, but the war brought a halt to the entertainment for a while, and the place was hired by the Yorkshire Electricity Board before, in September 1945, it re-opened as the News Theatre. Later, in January 1962, it became The Classic, and lasted as such for 20 years. An era had ended two years before a blaze in February 1984 rendered the property unsafe and it was demolished.

Meanwhile, across on the corner of Flat Street, the Odeon had already been a bingo house for more than a decade. Here was a cinema which had been planned in 1938, but, delayed by the war, was not built and opened until July 1956 – with the premiere of "Reach For The Sky". The biggest hits of the Odeon era were musicals "South Pacific", which ran for six months from Boxing Day 1958, and "The Sound of Music", which packed 'em in from October 1965 to February 1967. The last film was shown there in June 1971, and bingo became the name of the game.

The old Bell, like the old bank building on the bottom corner, has long since gone, but there is one story about this pub worth the telling, for here is where the racing career of Sheffield-born jockey and trainer, Harry Wragg, began. Harry's dad went in to the pub one night and struck up a conversation with a man who had come from Newmarket stables to collect a Sheffield youngster who had signed on to become a stable lad ...but the youngster had had a sudden change of heart. Harry's dad offered his son as a late substitute (Well, it was a time of high unemployment!) and the boy went on to earn fame and fortune, nicknamed "the Head Waiter" because he timed his push for the winning post with such perfection.

Lower High Street, peeping into Fitzalan Square. Note Marples on the right, and the old United Counties (later Barclays) Bank building at the junction with Commercial Street.

The Square after the 1909 improvements, but before the building of the Electra and the erection of the King Edward statue.

The Electra Palace and the King's statue are now in place.

A more modern view of the Square, when it was a tram terminus.

Star photographer Norman Allott captured this scene at the bottom of Norfolk Street in May 1964, before the dramatic changes prompted by the creation of Arundel Gate. Looking towards Fitzalan Square, on the left was Change Alley, while, across the road was Milk Street.

Just off the bottom of Norfolk Street was Milk Street, where, in the 19th century, there was a school called the Milk Street Academy.

Norfolk Street in the days when the YMCA was there. Legendary local benefactor, J.G.Graves, was a member here as a youngster, and he said it was there that he met friends who helped inspire him to launch his famous mail order business.

Inspecting the foundations of the new Victoria Hall in 1906 was turned into a social occasion by supporters of the venture and their families. The old Norfolk Street Wesleyan Chapel, which had existed from 1780, was demolished to make way for a splendid successor which was to be much more than just a religious centre.

The Victoria Hall, opened in September 1908, was a popular place for concerts and meetings from the outset, and those who appeared there included Sousa's Band, Paul Robeson and Paul Whiteman with his band, while there was one occasion in October 1932 when 3,000 people turned up to listen to Christopher Stone's special entertainment …a night of music on gramophone records!

That part of Norfolk Street behind the Town Hall, looking towards Howard Street and Union Street. These buildings went in the redevelopment which created the Town Hall extensions.

The other side of Norfolk Street, looking towards the Peace Gardens, the Town Hall and Surrey Street.

Just off Norfolk Street, across the road from the Peace Gardens, was the top of Howard Street and the premises of the famous old firm of Walker & Hall.

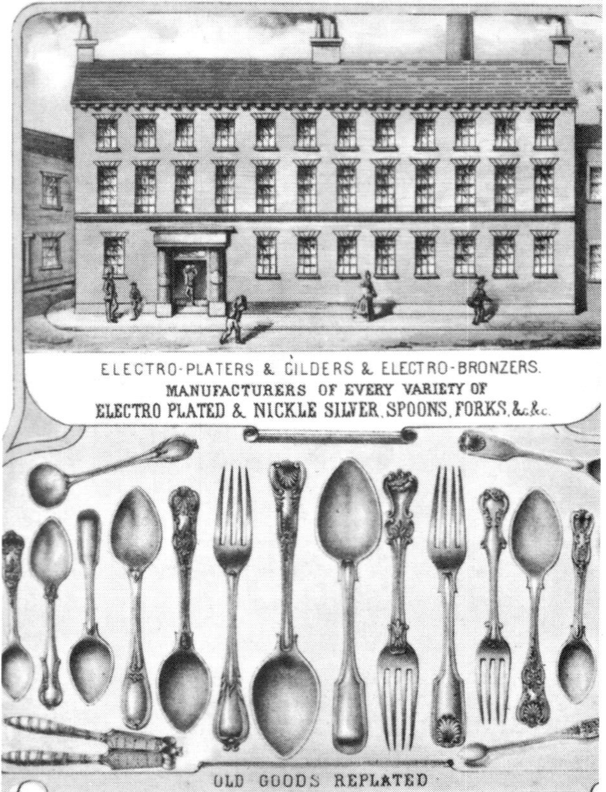

An old Walker & Hall advertisement.

This picture was taken close to the junction of St Paul's Parade, Norfolk Street and Union Street. The buildings on the far side of the street have long since disappeared.

Fargate …looking towards High Street.

Fargate …another view towards High Street, but spot the changes from the earlier picture.

Fargate ...the other side of the street. Chapel Walk is to the left, and the Marks & Spencer building replaced those at the heart of this picture, taken around 1905.

Fargate, at the top end, featuring the YMCA building and others situated between Norfolk Row and Surrey Street.

Looking down Fargate from Town Hall Square. On the left is the Monolith, which was later removed to Endcliffe Park. The Albany Hotel is on the right.

New Church Street, which ran between Pinstone Street and Norfolk Street, and disappeared when the Town Hall was built in the 1890s.

Pinstone Street of long ago.

What might be described as Vulcan's eye-view of the city, looking from the top of the Town Hall down Pinstone Street towards Moorhead. In the distance the tower of St Mary's Church, Bramall Lane.

An old print of Moorhead.

Old Button Lane and Moorhead, where properties disappeared in the redevelopments which brought new shops like Debenhams, the creation of the Grosvenor House Hotel, the opening of Charter Row, etc.

Another view of Moorhead in the snow, with Jay's furniture store and, to the right, Cambridge Street and the Hippodrome, the cinema which had begun life as a theatre.

Old Moorhead.

Looking down The Moor before redevelopments which transformed those ugly bombed sites into bright new stores and restored the area to its former popularity with shoppers.

Another view of The Moor, in between the wars.

The Moor in its Victorian heyday.

Town Hall Square, a shot from the end of Surrey Street looking across to Barker's Pool. The Queen Victoria Statue was erected in the square in 1905 and stayed there until 1930. The Cinema House, which opened in 1913, once entertained the famous comedians Laurel & Hardy, who came on a flying visit in 1932. The Wilson Peck premises on the corner remind us that this firm was created sometime in the early 1890s by John Peck and Arthur Wilson, though the latter's real name was Henry Mushet, of the steel family associated with Samuel Osborn's. Above the Cinema House are buildings demolished prior to the building of the City Hall.

Shops in old Barker's Pool.

Looking down from Barker's Pool, near the top of Cambridge Street, in that era when a public convenience and a horse trough stood not far from where the Cenotaph is now. The Albert Hall is down to the right.

Barker's Pool, looking down Division Street. Bottom right is the Ornamental Garden and Fountain at the corner of Balm Green, another of the gifts of J.G.Graves and opened in 1937; above that is the City Hall, opened in 1932, and, on the corner of Division Street and Holly Street, is the building which was once the home of the Graves' Mail Order empire. Across the road from that property is the Albert pub, which used to stand at the top of Cambridge Street. The white building across the road from the City Hall is Cole Brothers' new store, opened in the early 1960s.

The City Hall, floodlit. The foundation stone of this building was laid in 1929, and when it was completed it took away a lot of the concert and similar "business" of the Victoria Hall. Incidentally, one of the first "star" performers at the City Hall was a 15-year-old violin prodigy called Yehudi Menuhin. The Beatles appeared there in May 1963.

Parade at the War Memorial, Barker's Pool. This memorial was unveiled in October 1925 and almost immediately ran into heavy criticism. "The most unlovely war memorial in the entire country" said one critic, "like a disused telegraph pole" said another. The 108-foot mast, which weighs ten ton, was actually made in Hull, and, when it arrived in Sheffield at the old Wicker Goods Station, officials decided it would be safest to transport it up to Barker's Pool after midnight, when there would be less traffic on the streets.

Hoardings round the Ornamental Garden being created just above the Cinema House after J.G.Graves had made his gift, announced in late December 1936. The idea of the garden was that it would ensure the new City Hall would not be obscured on the bottom side by buildings. The property behind the garden site is the old Grand Hotel.

The end of Division Street, looking into Barker's Pool, in the days before the removal of properties to make way for the City Hall. On the left is the J.G.Graves' building, with the old Albert pub across the road on the corner of Cambridge Street.

A more modern view of the end of Division Street, taken after a parade past the War Memorial in Barker's Pool. The old Gaumont and Cole's new store can be seen, also the Albert pub, which dated from the 1870s and was demolished in the late 1970s.

West Street around 1904.

Fire Service parade, passing the Employment Exchange West Street, on the way back to the Division Street Station.

West Street, at the junction of Westfield Terrace.

West Street, near the junction with Fitzwilliam Street, around 1904.

Sheffield Fire Brigade, in the age of horse powered tenders, arriving back at the station in West Bar Green after dealing with an emergency.

The old Fire Brigade in the days of horse power were still a big attraction to local people.

Fire tenders of 1947 emerge from the Central Fire Station in Division Street.

Angel Street. Down on the left was the Angel public house, made famous by Sam Glanville, who launched a coach service to London from there.

Old Snig Hill.

A later view of old Snig Hill.

A steelworker bricked into the wall of this building in Castle Street.

York Street just before the buildings on the left were demolished ahead of the building of what became Kemsley House.

Old High Street.

Another view of High Street, circa 1880s.

Junction of York Street and High Street.

Lower end of High Street, looking towards Commercial Street.

Foot of High Street, looking upwards, with market on right.

Another view of the foot of High Street, with the C&A building on the right and Marples' on the left at the corner of Fitzalan Square.

The rebuilding of the Walsh's store in High Street.

A view of the foot of High Street showing the rebuilding on the site just below Change Alley and just above where the new Marples' pub was built.

Haymarket, looking towards Waingate and close to the junctions of Castle Street and Exchange Street. Wiley's, on the left, was a pub with an intriguing history, and the founder, old Wiley, was a remarkable man who advertised news in the pub window in the days before newspapers. When big cricket matches were staged up at Hyde Park, the scores were rushed to the Haymarket and everybody flocked to Wiley's window to see them. This little corner of the town, incidentally, witnessed great drama at the time of Sheffield first elections following the passing of the Reform Bill in 1832.

Looking up Haymarket in the era of the tram, with the Saturday shopping throng patiently waiting to cross the road.

Tramcar chaos in Haymarket, the Sheffield city centre thoroughfare once known as the Bull Stake.

The Sheffield Horse Repository, Castle Hill, nearly 90 years ago.

Buying vegetables and flowers from stallholders in Dixon Lane on a wet afternoon.

Victoria Hotel, Exchange Street-Furnival Road, circa 1910.

The old cattle market.

Hung …For A Joke On Lady's Bridge!

Lady's Bridge, being close to two well-known public houses and adjoining Waingate and the Wicker, has no doubt witnessed plenty of human drama in its time ….but nothing more tragic than the tale of two Sheffield button makers called John Stevens and Tom Lastley.

In 1790, at York, they were hung after a joke intended to humour a workmate called Wharton backfired on Lady's Bridge. Ironically, the trio had been in a party of five (the others were named Bingham and Booth) who had spent the day shopping and boozing together.

When Wharton put down his basket of groceries on the bridge and turned his back, the others picked it up and nipped over to the Barrel Inn in Pinstone Street, where they removed a leg of mutton and had it cooked. They said later that Wharton knew where they were going and had expected him to join them.

They were astonished when Wharton did not enjoy the joke, though he said later that Constable "Buggy" Eyre, to whom he had reported the theft, had insisted it was no laughing matter …there was £100 in "blood money" to be shared for a conviction. Thus, despite the four offering to replace the goods, they were arrested for highway robbery, and at York Assizes all except Bingham were sentenced to death – though Booth's sentence was subsequently commuted to transportation for life, and when he eventually received a pardon there were suspicions he had had a share of the "blood money".

The plight of the two men left in the shadow of the gallows prompted widespread sympathy in Sheffield, and the Master Cutler and several of the town's leading figures signed a petition. To their delight, news came from London that Stevens and Lastley had been granted a reprieve.

Alas, communications 200 years ago were painfully slow, so much so that the reprieve reached York two days after the men had been hung, protesting their innocence to the bitter end.

When a farewell letter penned by the men appeared in the local paper, outrage at the injustice knew no bounds, and Wharton's home in Bridgehouses was a target of a succession of attacks which left the house barely habitable. Wharton, scared for his life, escaped the mob by dressing in women's clothing and fleeing the town. He was never seen again.

The Lady's Bridge Hotel on the left. The buildings across the road were demolished to make way for the creation of Castlegate in 1930.

Another view of Lady's Bridge and the building which went to make way for the new road.

Bunting and barriers at Lady's Bridge and outside Tennant's Brewery and the public house, for the royal visit of 1905.

The Wicker

Times may have changed and taken much of the romance out of the Wicker, but it remains a thoroughfare with a fascinating history dating back to the days of the old Sheffield Castle … and much of what has happened there down the years echoes key stages in the city's development.

The Wicker was once the Assembly Green where the town's business was transacted and the people gathered on great occasions. One of these was the celebration of the passing of the Reform Bill in 1832, when 30,000 turned out with flags and musical instruments and paraded through the town. A less popular memory was when troops and people clashed at the height of Chartist activities in the 1840s.

The Wicker was used as a cattle market until the 1830s, and the annual summer and winter fairs were staged there. According to local folklore, in the 1590s cuckstools were a feature of the area: their purpose was as a chair complete with padlocks to imprison nagging wives, who were dipped in the River Don until they were cured!

With Sheffield's first railway station at the northern end of the Wicker from 1837, it was a place which witnessed many a memorable homecoming: such as when John Drury and other members of the Razor Grinders' Union, released from York Castle after a transportation sentence was overturned in 1847, arrived amid astonishing scenes. Through here, too, ran Sheffield's first horse tram (from Lady's

Bridge to Attercliffe) in 1873, and it was from the Wicker that the town's first omnibus ran. The place also boasted an early hospital (hence Spital Hill) and one of Sheffield's first post offices. It has often been recorded that, at the time of the Wars of the Roses, every man had to have a bow and arrow and practice on the Wicker butts. Soldiers from Sheffield Castle used the area for a similar purpose.

The name Wicker: where does it come from? Some say it was the wick yard of the Castle, others that the reeds which grew on the edges of the green, alongside the River Don, were used by the womenfolk to make wicker baskets. Yet it has been noted that such a broad meadow was invariably called a *ker*, and, after creation of the street in 1796 with the enclosure of the commons, local usage created Wicker.

The first building erected after that milestone was called the 'Sembly House, which was later pulled down and replaced by the Bull and Oak Inn, a pub once frequented by the poet James Montgomery.

Being a landlord was a popular but highly competitive business in the Wicker, for, in 1835, there were no fewer than ten pubs and beerhouses in the Street!

It was in the late 1840s that the district's most famous landmark was built: the 660-yard viaduct known as the Wicker Arches, created out of stone brought from Wharncliffe Crags, to serve the Sheffield & Manchester Railway line. The first train passed over the street in December 1848, and, within three years, a new passenger station, the Victoria, had been built to supersede Bridgehouses. In 1862 the station boasted a new hotel, which became the Royal Victoria and has survived long after the old line closed – and well beyond the era of the old Wicker Station which, ceasing as a passenger station with the building of the Midland Station in 1871, was for many years a goods depot. Just through the Arches in Savile Street was for many years the famous Bentley's garage.

The Wicker is gateway to the East End, where, from the 1850s, Sheffield's steel industry expanded at a tremendous pace, with the likes of Brightside, Attercliffe, Carbrook and Tinsley combining the growth of new industry with the extension of surburban housing often directly linked to the famous steel firms.

The Wicker had links with the Trades Union Outrages of the 1860s. There was a famous attempt to blow up a joiner's shop here in 1862, and a notorious shooting incident involving a non-union saw grinder in Nursery Street around the same period. The Tower

Wheel, just round the corner in Blonk Street, was a hotbed of non-union labour, and, as such, a frequent target for attack.

The area did not escape the Sheffield Flood of 1864. The clerk on night duty in the old Wicker goods yard was drowned. In Wicker Lane, poet

Richard Ryan claimed he had lost dozens of precious manuscripts in the disaster, including his Ode to John Brown's Armour Plate. He asked the court for £300 damages, but the Judge put their value at a mere £6...verse not being the most coveted commodity in such a down to earth district as "T'Wicker"!

The Wicker was also associated for many years with the cinema of the same name. This property, which no longer exists, had an unusual start, for, having been built as a picture palace, it was initially used as a steelworks warehouse. Not being quite finished when World War One started in 1914, plans to open it as a cinema were temporarily delayed... and the first film was not screened until June 1920. The cinema converted to sound in 1930 when the first "talkie" was *The Jazz Singer*, starring A1 Jolson. In October 1962 the Wicker was renamed Studio 7. In 1974 it became a three-in-one cinema. It closed in December 1982, re-opened briefly in 1986, but showed its last film in August 1987. Subsequently the building was demolished.

Familiar and Forgotten Buildings and Memorials

The surviving portion of the old Sheaf Works of Messrs Greaves. When opened in 1823 these premises were said to be Sheffield's first "proper" cutlery factory, in the sense that it brought all the various operations under a single roof.

The old gas offices in Commercial Street.

The one-time Coffee House in George Street, acquired by the Sheffield Banking Company in 1831.

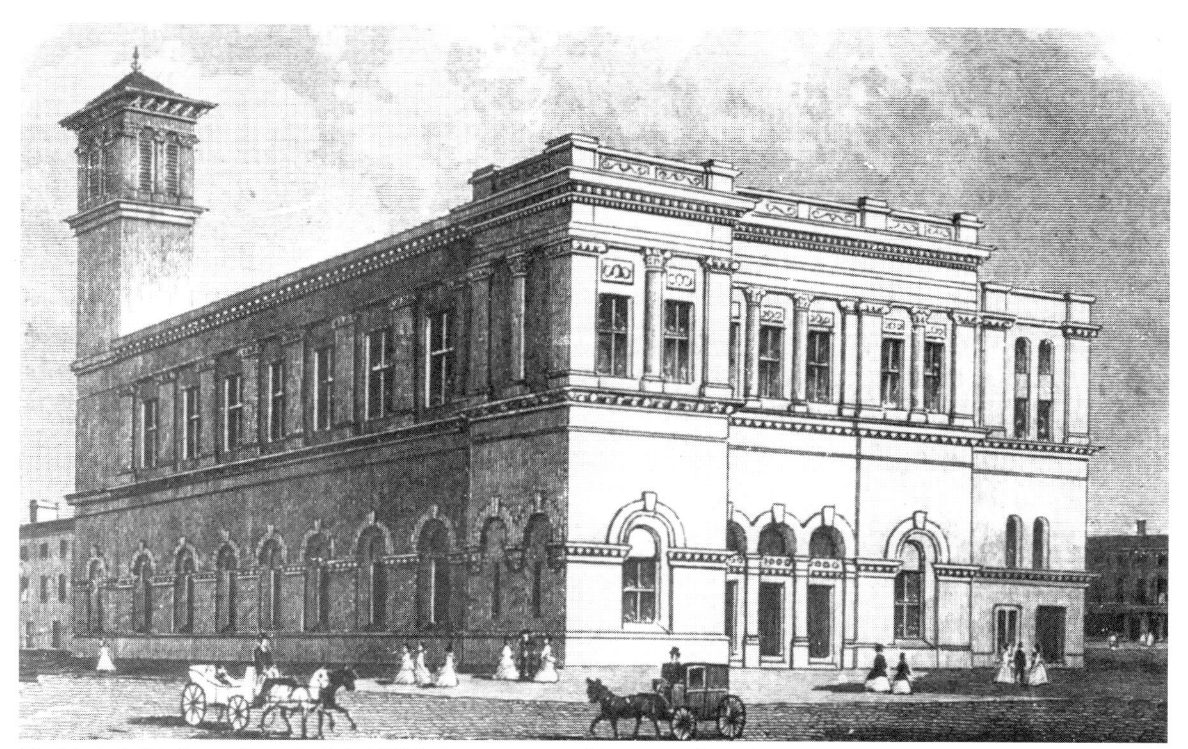

The Music Hall in Surrey Street, built in 1823. Its largest room could accommodate 1,000.

The King's Head in Change Alley. One of the many famous people who stayed here was Charles Dickens, a guest on his visits to perform at the Music Hall in Surrey Street.

The Albany Hotel, a temperance hotel which stood at the corner of Fargate and Surrey Street, was opened in October 1889.

The Barley Corn Inn, Cambridge Street.

Celebration time outside the Old Red House in Fargate on the occasion of the royal visit in 1905.

The old Packhorse Inn at the foot of Snig Hill. Behind it, to the left as you look at this picture, was the old Grand Theatre, originally known as the Bijou or New Star but re-opened as the Grand in June 1896. It had a spell as a cinema from 1912 to 1921, and was later used for exhibitions until it was demolished for road widening in 1938.

This building, which stood at the corner of Bank Street and Snig Hill, was the offices of the *Sheffield Independent* from 1846 to 1862.

This building, in Fargate, was demolished to make way for the Marks & Spencer store. It is of special interest because it was the last home of the *Sheffield Daily Independent,* for whom it was built in 1892.

Brunswick Chapel, which used to stand at the bottom of the Moor, dated back to 1834.

Cole Brothers was founded by three brothers in premises at the bottom of Fargate in 1847, and these premises were built around 1869. Cole's Corner was one of the city's most famous meeting places until the property was demolished after Cole's moved into new premises in Barker's Pool in 1963.

The Cole Brothers store in the process of demolition in the mid-1960s.

We had to use this picture of Castle Square, better known as "the Hole in the Road", because this famous landmark, opened in November 1967, was filled in during 1994 when work on laying the tracks for the new Supertram extension took the route up High Street.

There was a time when Sheffield boasted hundreds of industrial chimneys, but many have disappeared. This one was demolished in the early 1980s to facilitate redevelopments on Whitbread's Exchange Brewery site in Bridge Street.

The Lamp and Drinking Fountain, in Broad Lane, which is dedicated to the memory of the legendary James Montgomery.

The Crimean Memorial, which stood on Moorhead from the early 1860s to the late 1950s. The column was 58 feet high and the figure atop of it represented "Peace". This figure, minus the column, was re-erected in the Botanical Gardens.

The Monolith, a red polished obelisk, almost 390 feet high, was originally erected in Town Hall Square in February 1888 to mark Queen Victoria's Golden Jubilee a year earlier. It was removed to Endcliffe Park in 1904.

The Godfrey Sykes Monument in Weston Park.

OFFICIAL PROGRAMME,

Of The Royal Visit, May 21st. 1897.

The Queen, will arrive at the Midland station at 5, o'clock. Her Majesty will be received by His Grace the Duke of Norfolk, and several other prominent Citizens.

The Royal party will include 25 persons, who will be in attendence upon Her Majesty.

The Procession will leave the Station in the following order;—

The Chief Constable.

Mounted Police.

Troop of 17th. Lancers.

FIRST CARRIAGE,

The Honorary Secretaries,

SECOND CARRIAGE,

The Town Collector, The Master Cutler, The Deputy-Mayor, and Chairman of the Midland Railway Company,

THIRD CARRIAGE.

The Recorder, The Chairman of the Improvement Committee, the Town Clerk and General Manager of Midland Railway Company.

FOURTH CARRIAGE.

The Right Hon. A. J. Mundella, M. P. the Right Hon. C. Stuart Wortley, Q. C. M. P. Sir E. Ashmead Bartlett, M. P. & Sir C. E. Howard Vincent C. B. M. P.

FIFTH CARRIAGE,

The Lord Lieutenant and High Sheriff.

SIXTH CARRIAGE.

Lord Edmond Talbot M. P. and members of the Family of the Duke of Norfolk.

SEVENTH CARRIAGE.

The Mayor- His Grace the Duke of Norfolk, and the Lady Mary Howard.

Troop of the 17th. Lancers.

EIGHTH CARRIAGE.

Lieutanant F Ponsonby, Sir James Reid K. C. B, and Colonel Alfred Egerton.

NINTH CARRIAGE-

Miss Loch, the Hon. Ethel Cadogan, the Right Hon. Sir Matthew White Ridley M. P. Lieut-Colonel the Right Hon. Sir Fleetwood Edwards, K. C B.

TENTH CARRIAGE.

The Lady Southampton, the Hon. Mrs: Mallett. the Lord Chamberlain.

Escort of Her Majesty's 2nd: Life Guards,

HER MOST GRACIOUS MAJESTY

THE QUEEN.

H. R. H. The Princess Christian of Schleswig-Holstien: H. R. H. The Duke of Connought and Strathern. K. G.

The Queen's Enquerries.

The General Officers commanding the District.

Escort of Her Majesty 2nd. Life Guards.

Sheffield Squadron of the Yorkshire Dragoons.

Yeomanry Cavalry.

Mounted Police.

The route to the Town Hall is to be along Sheaf Street, Commercial Street, High Street, Fargate, Surrey Street Norfolk Street, Upper Charles Street, and Pinstone Street.

The ceremony outside the front entrance of the Town Hall, will occupy 10, to 12, minutes, here a guard of the Ist. Hallamshire Volunteer Battalion, York and Lancaster Regiment, will take up their position as guard of honours.

The Queen will remain in her carriage through out the ceremony. The Duke of Norfolk will present an address from the Corporation, enclosed in the beautiful golden casket manufactured by Messrs. Mappin and Webb an address will also be handed to Her Majesty from the Cutlers' Company and the Town Trustees. Her Majesty having handed written replies, will by a electrical arrangment, open the large front gates of the Town Hall.

On leaving the Town Hall the route will be by Barker's Pool, Cambridge Street. South Street Moor, Hereford Street, St. Mary's Road, Farm Road and Norfolk Park Road to Norfolk Park, where the 4th. West Riding Yorks. Volunteers artillery will act as Her Majesty's guard of honour.

As the Royal procession enters the park, the children will sing the National Anthem accompained by the bands, Dr. Coward officiating as conductor.

On reacing the childrens stands the Royal carriage will be drawn up in position to enable Her Majesty to have a good view of the little ones; the children will then sing two more hymns, after which the Queen will drive between the two stands on which the children will be grouped, the children singing "Rule Britainia" on the departure of Her Majesty.

On leaving Norfolk Park, Her Majesty will travel along Norfolk Road, South St. Broad Street, Corn Exchange, Furnival Street, Blonk Street, the Wicker and Savile Street, to Messrs. Chas. Cammell & Co's, Ltd. Cyclops Works.

At these works a special carriage way will be made over the Midland goods line to the armour plate department, where Her Majesty's carriage will be drawn up at some distance from the rolls. Everything will be in readiness for the rolling of the plate, and it is contemplated that the Queen's stay within the Cyclops works will not exceed ten minutes, The plate having been rolled, Her Majesty's carriage will turn towards the Midland goods lineand will draw up at a temporary platform where the Royal train will be in waiting.

Her Majesty's departure is fixed for 7, o'clock precisely, thus giving exactly two hours for the whole visit, including three ceremonies and a journey of six miles.

The entire route will be lined with Military and the Crimean and Indian Veterans of the district, will mount guard at the Crimean Monument.

Official programme of Queen Victoria's visit to Sheffield in 1897, when Her Majesty stayed for barely two hours – just long enough to officially open the new Town Hall, look in at Norfolk Park, and see some armour plate rolled in the Cyclops Works of Charles Cammell & Co.

Surburban Sheffield

A tramcar climbs the steep incline of Duke Street in the era before those shops and houses were demolished as part of the Park Hill redevelopment. At the bottom of the hill, just round the corner, was Gunstone's Bakery; across the road from that, the Canal Wharf buildings, and you can see over the Duke Street rooftops the tower of the old Corn Exchange. The area at the foot of this hill was transformed with the creation of the Park Square roundabout and the Parkway link with the Motorway.

Jimmy Young's shop at the corner of Lord Street and Talbot Street, with all those sweets and goodies displayed in the window, was a wonderful attraction for children in that corner of the Park district ...and don't those old signs for Lyons' Tea, Horniman's Tea, and Cherry Boot Polish (not to overlook the poster for the Norfolk Cinema) evoke some good old memories?

The ruins of Manor Castle, inevitably linked with Mary, Queen of Scots.

Cemetery Avenue, off Ecclesall Road.

Hodgson Street.

Washday in one of the courtyards behind Hodgson Street.

Collegiate Crescent, off Ecclesall Road.

Hunters Bar.

An old print of Ecclesall Church.

Banner Cross Hall.

Nether Green.

London Road.

The old Abbeydale Toll Bar.

Abbeydale Road, near Chippinghouse Road, about 100 years ago.

Building the swimming pool at Millhouses Park.

There has always been something of a mystery about why Psalter Lane should boast a silent "P", but, apparently, before the extra letter was added, there was this building known as "the salt box" because it was thought to resemble a salt container.

This picture was taken in Dore High Street in 1906, and one of the girls featured in it is Nellie Flint, who often recalled that her father was secretary of the now long-forgotten Dore & Totley Sick & Funeral Society. The members of this organisation used to meet every August Bank Holiday Monday in the Hare & Hounds, then, led by the Dore Brass Band, march up to the Cross Scythes at Totley.

Empire Day celebrations in Shoreham Street.

The bottom of Clough Road, houses which have long since gone.

London Road, just beyond Highfields.

Lowfield.

Top of Heeley Green.

Heeley

Old Catch Bar, Heeley

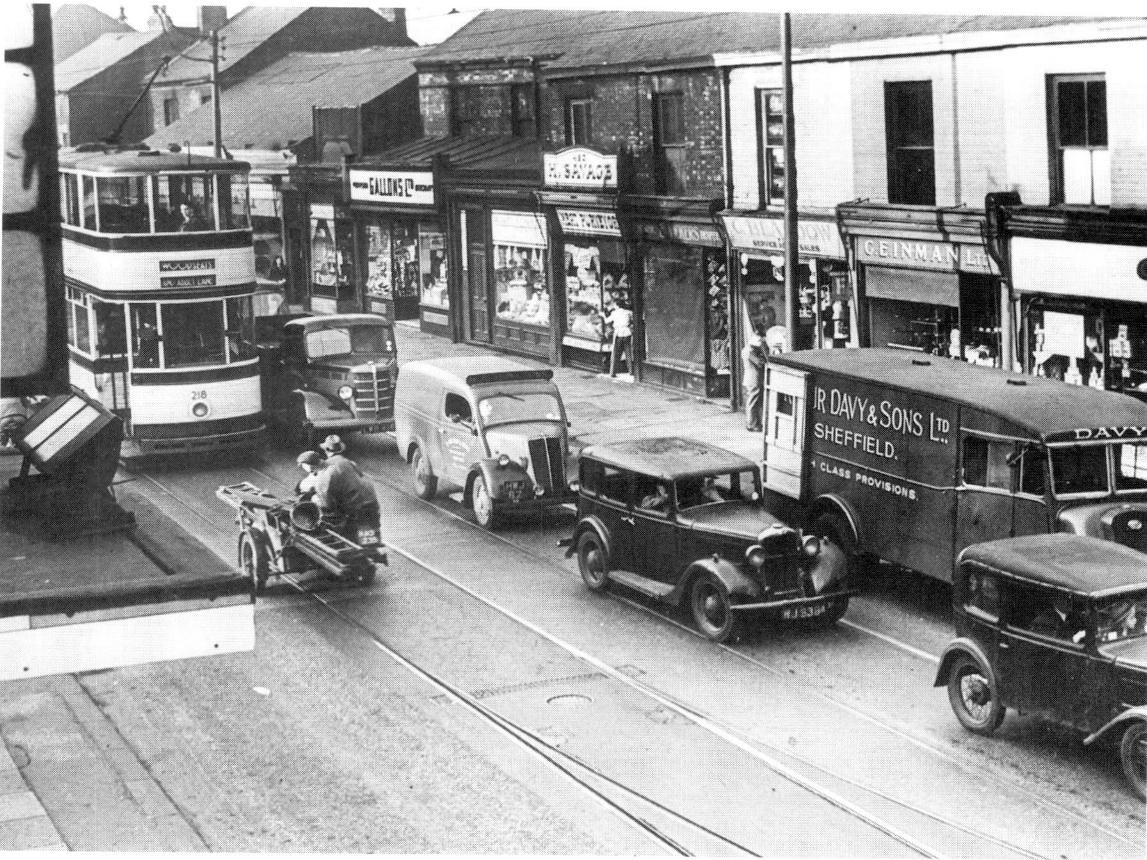

Heeley

Drama near the junction with Derbyshire Lane as Woodseats tramcar overturns after crash involving a lorry on the Chesterfield Road.

Aeriel view of Woodseats.

Old Woodseats.

Old Hall, Norton Lees.

A Pauline Shearstone drawing of Oakes Park, Norton.

Norton Parish Church, By Pauline Shearstone.

On the farm at Norton lane.

Hill Top at Gleadless, featuring, up the road, the Ball Inn, reputed to be a regular haunt of "Swift Nick", the highwayman. (From Pauline Shearstone's "Gleadless from Village to Suburb")

The Old Harrow, White Lane, Gleadless, as it was in 1911.

Myrtle Springs Toll Bar, which was situated at the top of Gleadless Road. Demolished in the 1960s. Drawing by Pauline Shearstone.

Crosspool School.

Whit Walk up Western Bank.

Western Bank, just below the University, as it was.

Winter Street Hospital, opened 1881.

Walkley tram terminus 1904.

Looking towards Crookesmoor and Crookes from Netherthorpe.

School Road tram depot.

19th-century drawing of Commonside, Crookes.

An illustration which captures a scene alongside the Don on Penistone Road in the early 19th century. Note the soldier out a courting, presumably from the original barracks, which were situated between the Penistone and Infirmary Roads – just south of Hillfoot Bridge.

A view looking towards Hillfoot Bridge and towards the city centre before the houses were demolished. The Kelvin flats can be seen (top, right). Incidentally, in 1994, despite all the changes in this area, some of those old pigeon huts still survive.

Owlerton Hall.

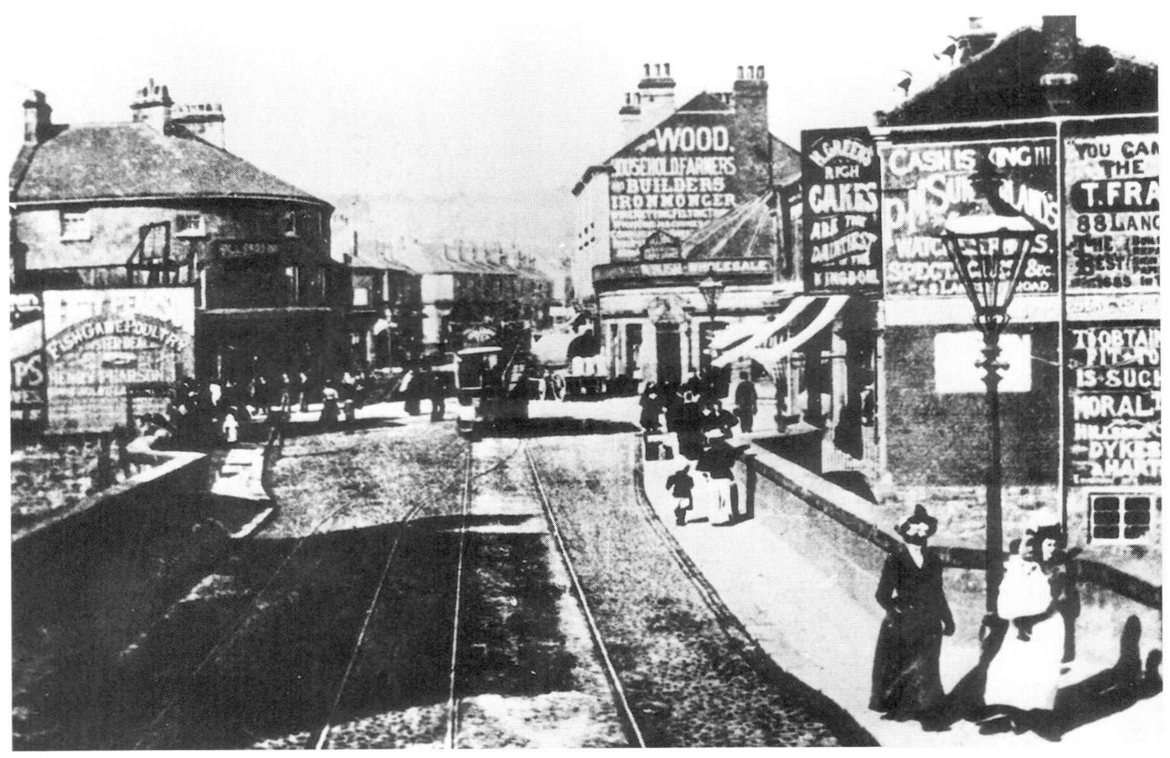

Hillsborough Corner.

Isaac Shires' pub at Hillsborough Corner.

Middlewood Road at the junction with Dykes Hall Road.

Middlewood Road.

Tram stuck in the snow, Parkside Road-Middlewood Road.

Outing from the Middlewood Tavern in the early 1920s.

Millhouses Station.

Heeley Station.

Beauchief Station, closed January 1961.

The junction of Rock Street and Pitsmoor Road, a picture probably taken when the buildings marked with an "x" (and the chapel on the right which you cannot quite see) were due for demolition ahead of making the bridge over the railway. On the left of the gaslamp you can just pick out the top of Macro Street, which dipped down alongside the railway as far as the bridge over Woodside Lane. Incidentally, down at the bottom of Macro Street, number 78 was the old Wellington Inn and converted into a lodging house run by Ma Easy. All long since gone.

Looking up Woodside Lane in late 1957 a year or so prior to the demolition of the houses.

Pye Bank School, high on the hill at the top of Andover Street and at the back looking down on Pitsmoor road.

The White building was a chip shop, situated on Andover Street, just off Rock Street, and said to be a house dating from Tudor times. Over the rooftops, evidence of high-rise modern flats, all part of the Woodside-Pye Bank redevelopment.

Burngreave Cemetery, a picture taken from Danville Mount. This part of the cemetery is by the Melrose Road entrance, but the site extends right over to Scott Road and could be the largest burial ground in Sheffield.

Abbeyfield House in Abbeyfield Park.

The famous unusual shaped Toll House at the junction of Pitsmoor Road and Burngreave Road.

Pye Bank Tower.

Beyond Firshill, going down the Barnsley Road towards Firvale, with St Cuthbert's and the old Methodist Church in the valley. Down the hill to the right was the Sunbeam Cinema (now a petrol station is on the site), and if you go to the right at the bottom, you come to Owler Lane. Straight ahead and you reach Firth Park, or, if you continue up Barnsley Road across the dip, you will come to Sheffield Lane Top.

Firth Park, close to the junction of Sicey Avenue and Bellhouse Road. The old Methodist Church is still there. The picture was taken in the heyday of the old trams, which ran straight through the middle of the roundabout!

Who can remember a pond in Firth Park?

This is Windmill Lane, probably just before 1914, when the area at the top of Bellhouse Road was being developed into one of the best known Council estates on that side of the city.

Longley Park swimming baths, which date from just before World War Two. The park and pool were always popular with people from Southey and surrounding districts, the open spaces being close enough to Sheffield Lane Top, Firth Park and parts of Parson Cross.

The Old Ecclesfield Parish of Alfred Gatty

Ecclesfield may have changed a great deal in modern times, but the famous old church, once called "the Minster of the Moors", still dominates a village which is now a suburb of Sheffield, and it continues to evoke memories of the legendary Dr Alfred Gatty, the most famous and longest-serving vicar in the history of a parish which once spanned a staggering 78 square miles and included Wadsley Bridge, Grenoside, Chapeltown and Oughtibridge.

Gatty, who arrived in Ecclesfield in 1839 and stayed until his death in 1903, was a remarkable man, not content to administer his huge parish, but was author of several books and edited the 1875 edition of Hunter's Hallamshire. His wife, Margaret Scott, was the daughter of Nelson's chaplain (who had cradled the dying Admiral in his arms at Trafalgar), while their own second daughter, Juliana Ewing, earned fame as a children's author, and, indeed, her invention of the Brownies in one tale inspired the Baden-Powell to create the real-life junior branch of the Girl Guide movement.

Gatty, ordained in 1837, met his wife while a curate at Bellerby in North Yorkshire. Coincidentally, Margaret's uncle, Thomas Ryder, was Vicar of Ecclesfield, and when he died soon after the Gattys' marriage, Alfred was offered the living in which he became a South Yorkshire legend.

They arrived by stage coach, and it says much about the pre-railway world of over 150 years ago that their furniture was brought by canal to Masbro' Wharf and then carted by road to a village famous for its fork, nail and gimlet making – and notorious for its sporting enthusiasm for bull and bear baiting and dog and cock fighting.

Another activity the villagers enjoyed was watching chained prisoners pass along Ecclesfield Common en route to Wakefield after sentence by Sheffield magistrates. Local wrongdoers were still likely to find themselves in the stocks in Stocks Hill – a spot now dominated by three pubs, but still regarded with affectionate memories from many years of Whit Sings.

Yet while Gatty found the village "rude and rough" and his background such a contrast with that of his parishioners, he had the knack of being able to mix with the poorest of them as easily as with the Earl Fitzwilliam up at Wentworth. And, as he said in his autobiographical "A life at One Living", there was more to praise about the district than to criticise.

The rambling old vicarage (in which the children were born to the Gattys) was demolished in the 1960s, and, indeed, so much of old Ecclesfield has disappeared in modern times ...like the Rawson school, many once-familiar cottages, etc. Yet some buildings from his era survive, and his name lives on in the Gatty Memorial Hall, built 90 years ago soon after his death.

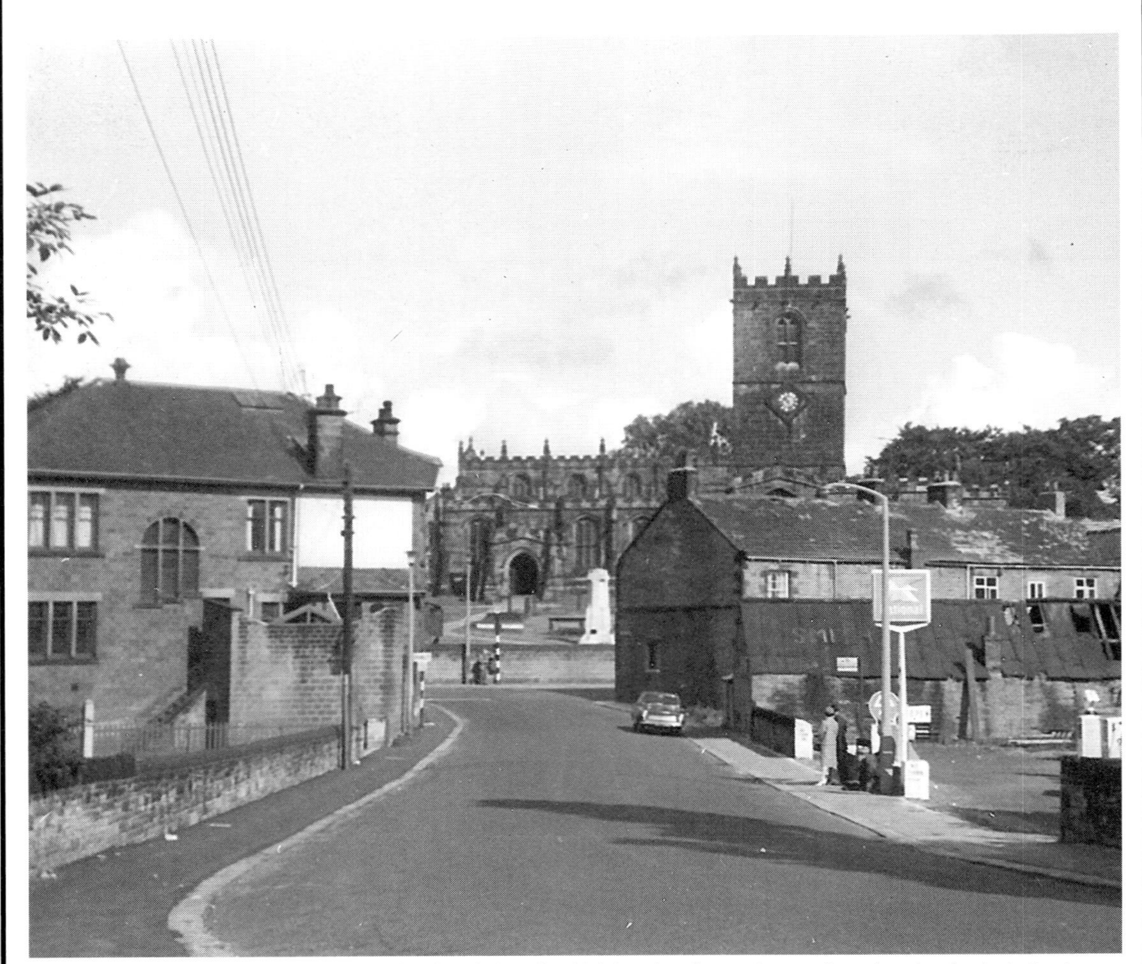

Ecclesfield Church. The building on the left is the Black Bull, which is only a few yards away from the trio of pubs in Stocks Hill Square.

Ecclesfield Priory.

Ye Olde Tankard in Stocks Hill is now known as The Stocks, and what was the post office alongside is now a hairdressing salon.

Whitley Hall. This old mansion, which probably dates back 400 years, once belonged to the Parker and Shirecliffe families, and later came into the possession of William Bingley, and while it belonged to the Bingleys it was a boarding school run by John Rider. In modern times it has been a conference centre, and today is an excellent hotel and restaurant. Incidentally, not too far from the old mansion is the delightful little Whitley Hall cricket ground, a place long synonymous with "Ike" Baxter.

Up top end of Grenoside.

Grenoside, at the bottom side, on the main road to and from Sheffield.

Up top of Lound Side, Chapeltown.

The famous Five Arches on Herries Road, near the Wednesday FC ground, carrying a train from Sheffield bound for Manchester.

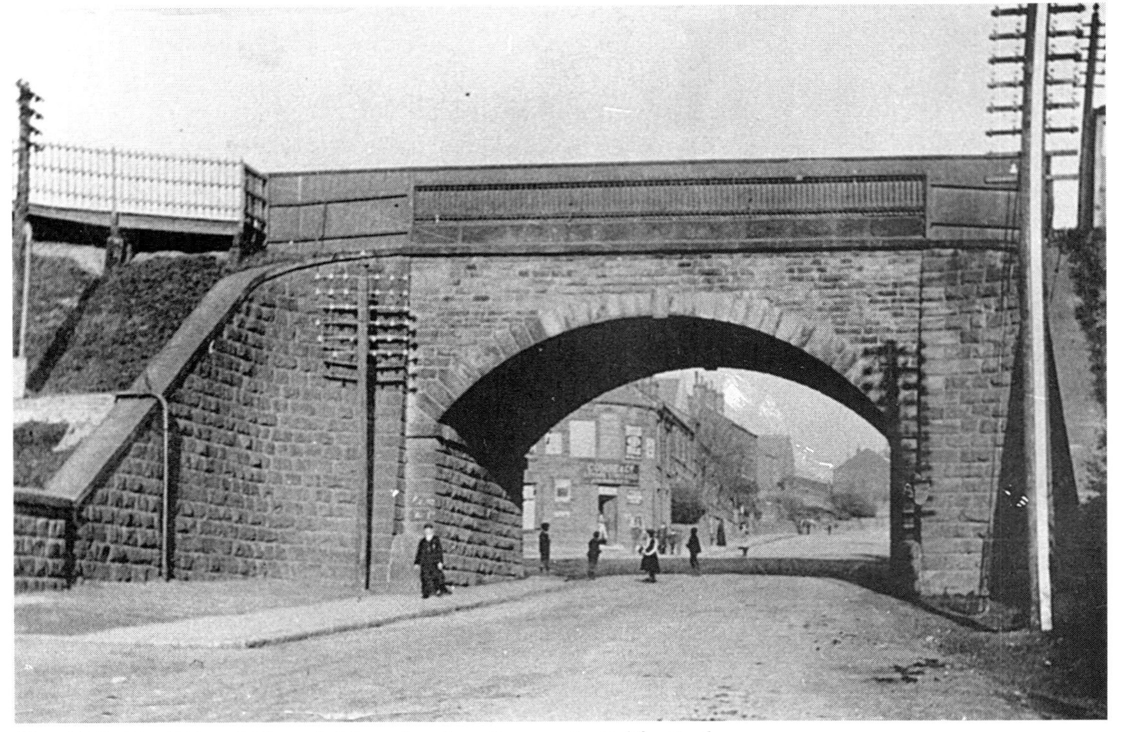

The old Wadsley Bridge which carried the early railway line over the Halifax Road.

The main road at Wadsley Bridge, where Penistone Road North becomes Halifax Road.

Wadsley Old School, built by subscription in 1800.

Oughtibridge around 1905.

A Whitsuntide gathering at Oughtibridge more than 80 years ago.

A pleasing view of old Oughtibridge.

Passing trams at Norfolk Bridge.

Old Attercliffe, near the famous old Palace Theatre, in the days when tradesmen's transport used a kind of horse-power not quite so familiar in modern times!

Another view of Attercliffe, probably just before World War One.

Maltby Street School (the building is still standing in 1994) was one of the newer schools in the Attercliffe area, having opened in January 1922, and it offered the novelty of shower baths for pupils. Indeed pupils from other schools used these facilities, and very pleased their mothers were, too, for this was in an era when few East End houses boasted bathrooms and it was more common for families to fetch the tin bath in from the yard, boil water in pans on the open fire or gas ring, lock all the doors, and make the kids take turns to have a good scrub!

Old Cottages near the Attercliffe Vestry Hall.

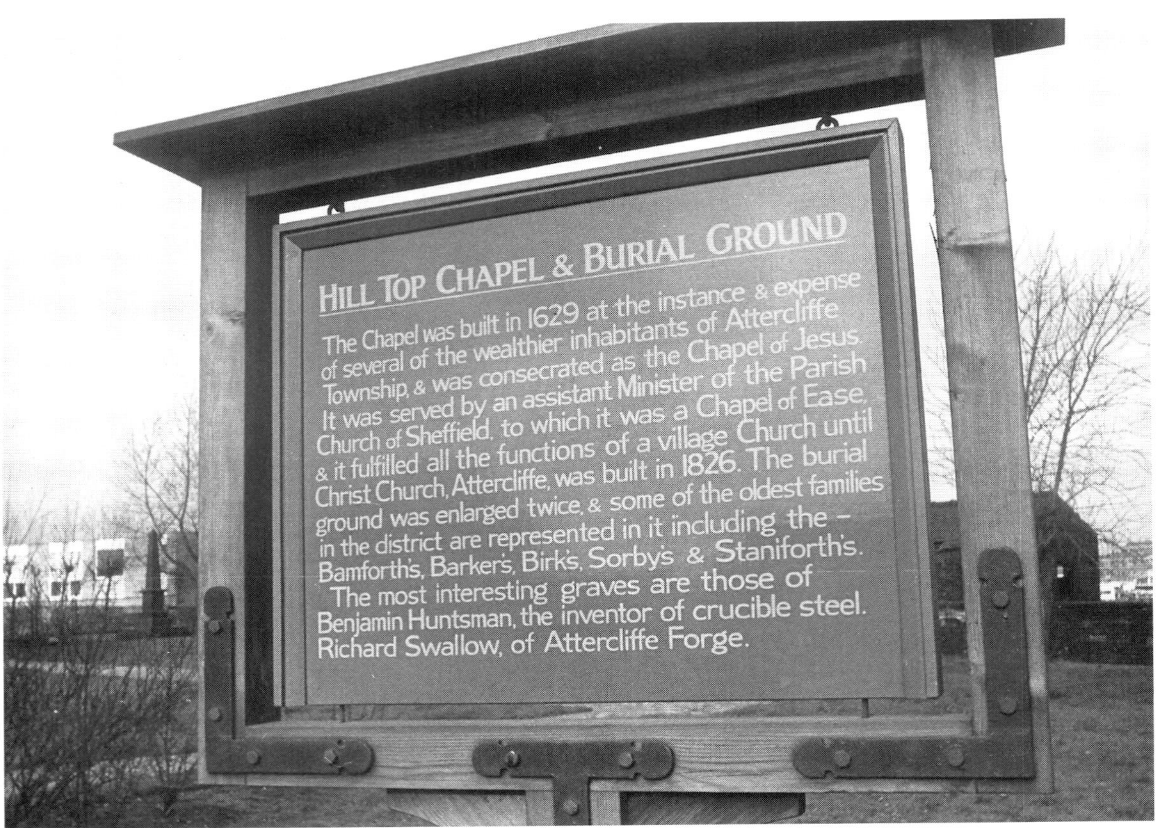

The sign at Hill Top burial ground on Attercliffe Common reminds us that some famous Sheffield men were laid to rest here, including Benjamin Huntsman, the inventor of crucible steel.

The Attercliffe works of Benjamin Huntsman, who came to Sheffield and sought to find a formula for making steel ideal for his clockmaking …and discovered a crucible steel which, though local cutlers did not take to it immediately, was to have a dramatic impact on Sheffield trades and the town's reputation for the best in cutlery and tools.

Carbrook Church.

Carbrook School, which opened in August 1874 and gave good service to the local community until the demolition of all the houses in the district.

The Pheasant Inn at Carbrook. There was once a football pitch behind this pub, and it was here in the late 1890s that Sheffield Wednesday once nearly acquired land for a new ground. In the event, they went to Owlerton instead!

The old Tinsley tram depot, which stood at the junction of Weedon Street and Attercliffe Common – an ideal site for ensuring there were plenty of trams to get the workers home from the steelworks which once dominated the district.

The advertisement for Stones Ales on the side of this house in Sheffield Road, Tinsley, and the sign outside the shop for the same brew, served to confirm that they had an affection for local beer in the heart of the old East End!

Wincobank Castle.

An aerial view of the Tinsley Viaduct and the Meadowhall and Wincobank areas. Those familiar landmarks, the two gasholders at Wincobank and the twin cooling towers of the old Blackburn Meadows Power Station, remain in 1994, but the steelworks have gone and the area is now dominated by the Meadowhall Shopping complex.

A view across the Meadowhall section of the Lower Don Valley in the days when steam trains still ran and so many famous old steel firms thrived in the district.

Meadowhall and Wincobank Station as it was.

The modern Meadowhall Station, catering for both Inter-City trains and Supertram, and, with a bus terminal close by and the Tinsley Viaduct carrying the M1 motorway right across the valley, there is not much doubt that the new Meadowhall shopping complex is well served with routes to ensure the customers can get there!

Children gather in the yard of a cottage in Darnall Square, sometime around 1912.

Darnall terminus in the era of the open topped tramcar.

Broughton Lane in 1994 is rather different from what it was when this picture was taken by *Star* photographer Arthur Benjamin in the early 1970s, for where these houses stood you will now find the Sheffield Arena site.

This drawing is intended to illustrate how Attercliffe Common looked around the beginning of the 19th century, showing the Arrow Inn, Carbrook Hall and the gibbet on which the body of the man who gave Broughton Lane its name was allowed to hang on public view from 1792 until 1827 – the spectacle attracting thousands of curious visitors from miles around and turning the Arrow into one of the most profitable pubs in the region. Spence Broughton has passed into folklore as the man who, with his pal John Oxley, robbed a post boy on the Sheffield to Rotherham road at Ickles. They got away with only a few pounds, but Oxley subsequently "shopped" Broughton and, at York Assizes, the judge decided to make an example of him, declaring that not only should Broughton be hanged but his body then be suspended from a gibbet to deter others from pursuing a life of crime. When Broughton's body arrived in the East End, it was estimated that at least 40,000 people turned up to see it on the first day, and the occasion was more like a carnival than a wake. The gibbet became a landmark, Broughton a martyr, and, when a new lane was made near the spot, it was called after a highwayman who only achieved fame by virtue of the circumstances in which he died and the fact that his remains became an amusing spectacle to the crowds.

A tremendously popular event in the East End in the old days was the annual Darnall Medical Aid parade. Here the floats make their way up Staniforth Road.

Industrial Sheffield

The Bridgefield Works of Samuel Newbould were situated at the bottom of Little Sheffield Moor, and were occupied by the firm from 1784 until the transfer to Newhall Road in 1871, The firm eventually amalgamated with Sanderson Brothers, and later still the business became Sanderson Kayser Ltd.

Demolition of the Leeds Road works of Brown Bayley's, the site upon which the Don Valley Stadium was built.

Demolition of the old Carlisle Works of Sanderson Kayser in the mid 1980s.

The former Jessop's works at Brightside.

Hadfield's East Hecla Work before demolition, This is the area which was subsequently redeveloped to create the Meadowhall Shopping Centre.

The old Richards cutlery works, near the Moorfoot, during demolition.

The Stella Works of W.A.Tyzack during demolition.

The junction of Savile Street East and Sutherland Street, featuring the water tower which was once something of a landmark in the district before the demolition of the old Firth Brown premises.

Forging a hollow marine shaft under a 2,000-ton press at Firth's Norfolk Works.

Cores of the famous 12,000 and 22,000-pound bombs made at the Vickers Works of the English Steel Corporation in wartime Sheffield.

A 110-ton hollow gun tube forged at Firth's Norfolk Works.

A scene in the file hardening shop at Firth's Norfolk Works.

Hydraulic press used for bending armour plate in Cammell's Cyclops Works.

A 6,000-ton hydraulic forging press at Camell's Grimesthorpe Works.

Steelmaking at Firth Brown's.

Old style haulage contractor from the Owlerton district of Sheffield.

The days when the womenfolk answered the country's call for labour and helped produce shells in Sheffield steelworks during World War One.

Emergency edition of the Sheffield Independent in May 1926 during the General Strike.

SHEFFIELD INDEPENDENT

EMERGENCY EDITION

No.22,336 Thursday, 6 May, 1926, One Penny X

GENERAL POSITION.- No important change. In Commons yesterday Mr. Henderson appealed for return last Monday's position. Newcastle City Council urge withdrawal general strike order, re-opening mines on existing terms with continuance of subsidy until settlement. Ministry of Transport ask car owners willing to give pedestrians lift to show their destination.

DISORDERLY INCIDENTS.- Police charged London crowd attempting stop delivery of Government's newspaper. Three tramcars attacked by Leeds strikers, passengers injured. Police attack repulsed. Crowd, 6,000, attacked bus at Stoke, police use batons. Three motor vehicles set alight in London, many disabled. Driver of bus at Birmingham roughly handled by crowd, conductor hit with spanner.

FOREIGN ITEMS.- German Trade Unions decided measures thwart shipment of coal to England. Similiar call to French workmen. Miners' International Committee meet Ostend Saturday.

SHEFFIELD.- Carters assaulted in Sorby street, two arrests. William Whitham, Corporation bus driver, remanded charge assaulting Arthur Kitson, bus owner, Kitson's arm broken. Cutlery and grinding trades notified not affected by strike.. A Voluntary Service Committee arranging motor "lifts" for workpeople. General Manager Tramways announced plenty volunteers ready; refused to say if volunteer service will be run. ABBEY LANE TRAMS: Sheffield City Council approved scheme to run tramway extension in Abbey lane.

RACING.- Chester Executive decided no racing at Chester to-day. Chester Returns: 2.0, 1 Jennie Deans (1-7), 2 Semiramis (7-1); 2.30, 1 Little Grev (10-11), 2 Horace ([illegible]-1), 3 Red Ronald (6-1); 3.15, 1 Midennis (11-2), 2 Vermilion Pencil (4-1), 3 Ixia (10-1); 3.50, 1 Napths (2-1), 2 Grippeminaud (7-4), 3 The Merchant (4-1); 4.20, 1 Arc-en-ciel (3-1), 2 Dusky Brave (1-3); 5.20, 1 Maritza f (2-5), 2 Fun (5-2).

BILLIARDS.- Interval scores: Smith (in play), 3,750, Davis 4,322; F.Oates (in play) 502, A.E.Tingle 492.

CRICKET CLOSE.- No play yesterday- Surrey v Glamorgan; Essex v Australians. Yorkshire 176 Cantabs 118 for 4. Worcester 115 for 4 v Lancs.

GOLF.- Hallamshire won Sheffield Unions second team competition at Abbeydale with 735 aggregate. Abbeydale 760; Hillsbro 766. H.Henderson (Hillsbro) won Yorkshire Golf Professional Tournament beating A.McKenzie (Ilkley) 7 and 5.

FOOTBALL.- Rotherham United re-signed E.F.Lievesley, centre forward, and secured G.Bayliss, halfback. So far there is no liklihood of of F.A.tour to Canada being cancelled.

LONDON STOCK EXCHANGE.- Few changes, mainly falls. Gilt edged easier. Mines and rubbers unchanged. Armstrongs and Babcocks slightly better. Some oils marked down.

TROOP MOVEMENTS.- Large numbers fully equipped troops in charabancs travelling north through Doncaster received good natured banter from crowds of strikers.

TO-DAY'S WEATHER.- Fair generally, with possibility of some light showers, moderate temperature and light wind.

Workmen at Thomas Glossop's Harmer Lane works around 1901, the occasion prompting the photograph apparently being the coming of age of the boss's son, young Billy (in bowler hat).

A group of Newton Chambers old-timers on the occasion of their retirement from the firm in the 1950s.

Tommy Hoyland, of Ecclesfield, was one of the many characters of the old Thorncliffe Works of Newton Chambers, where he worked as a blacksmith from 1895 to 1954 – a 59-year spell during which he saw great changes. When he started work, the normal hours were from 6am to 9pm, and, after completing his apprenticeship he could earn 34 shillings (£1.70) a week. That doesn't sound much, but flour was 10d (4p) a stone and coal 7d (3p) a bag at the time. And, by the way, Tommy (he died in 1961) said he always walked to work because it was too early for public transport, and, anyway, he couldn't be wasting his hard-earned money on bus fares!

This picture, taken in the machine shop of the famous old Chapeltown firm of Newton Chambers over 70 years ago, has been loaned by one of the young apprentices featured in it, and he was saying that it evokes an era when work suddenly became hard to get. "The minute you had served your time (in my case as an engineer) and were due for stepping into the 'senior' ranks, a firm made you redundant and brought in more youngsters," he said. "I ended up having to go down the pit at Thorpe Hesley, and didn't get back into engineering until well after the 1926 strike, when I found employment at Brightside Engineering's Ecclesfield factory. But even then I had to begin again as a labourer and wait for the chance to get back into my trade. It was just the way things were and you had to accept it."

Newton Chambers in its Thorncliffe heyday was a firm which pioneered the concept of its own college for young employees, and this 1954 picture is of girls who were beginning their careers, learning shorthand and typing with a view to becoming secretaries. The principal was Miss Mary Berry, a legendary figure in the firm's post-war history.

A group of young East Enders unemployed and looking for work in the 1930s.

Editorial department of the *Sheffield Telegraph* and *Star* in that era before even typewriters were familiar aids to the art of journalism.

Putting *The Star* "to bed", 1948. A typical scene on what they call "the stone" in that newspaper era now referred to as "the hot metal days".

Men at work in *The Star's* composing room, setting reporters' "copy" in type, in 1963.

A section of *The Star's* editorial room in the early 1960s, with the news sub editors on the left and the sports staff on the right.

Sporting Sheffield

Sheffield's Crucible Theatre has been synonymous with the World Snooker Championships since 1977, when John Spencer beat Cliff Thorburn in the Final. This picture captures the 1979 semi-final in which Dennis Taylor defeated John Virgo before going on to lose to Terry Griffiths in the Final. This annual sports event serves to remind us that the Crucible, which replaced the old Playhouse in 1971, was built on the site of the famous sporting pub, the Adelphi, which stood at the corner of Arundel Street and Sycamore Street and was the place which hosted the meetings at which the decisions to build Bramall Lane (1854) and to form Yorkshire CCC (1863) and Sheffield Wednesday FC (1867) were taken.

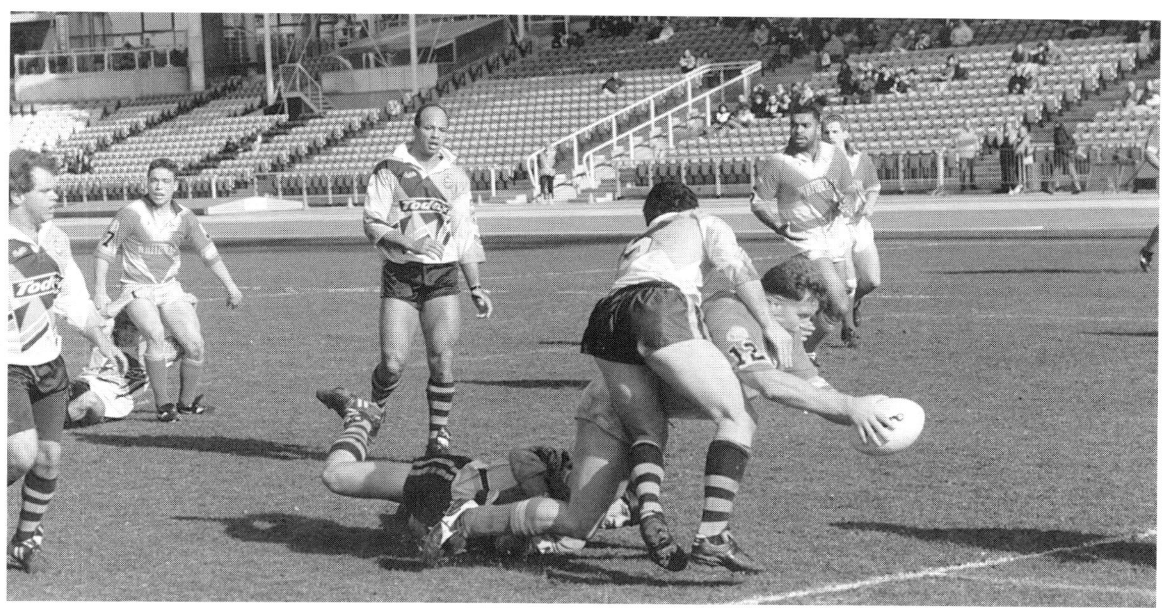

The Don Valley Stadium, built on the site of the famous old Brown Bayley steelworks at the start of the 1990s, had a key role in attempts to breathe new life into Sheffield's East End following the decline of traditional industries, and the aim of promoting Sheffield as a sporting city was at the heart of plans to regenerate the city's economy. The stadium has become synonymous with major athletics events, but, appropriately perhaps, it is also the home of Sheffield Eagles RLFC, whose emergence in modern times has added another string to the city's sporting bow. Although a Rugby League 'international' was staged at Bramall Lane as long ago as 1911, this was not a sport readily associated with a traditional soccer stronghold ...but then Gary Hetherington and his Eagles flew in and made an immediate hit.

Another "new" sport which has really taken off in the city in recent times has been ice hockey, with Sheffield Steelers attracting a big and enthusiastic following to their matches at the Sheffield Arena – another major development in the city's East End.
This picture features action in an England v Scotland junior ice hockey international in November 1991. The Arena, which is situated on Broughton Lane, off Attercliffe Common, is now a famous venue for "big" concerts which attract the world's top stars.

Since the Sheffield Sports Stadium opened at Owlerton in the late 1920s, it has staged a remarkable variety of sports. The place is synonymous with greyhound racing and speedway, but soccer, rugby, athletics and even horse racing have been staged there ...and this picture from August 1983 features the Stock Car World Championships.

Ponds Forge as it was ...for years the headquarters of George Senior & Sons. Old George, who was a famous civic and industrial figure in his time and one of Sheffield's most successful self-made men, would have been saddened at the turn of events which precipitated the demise of the old firm. However, he was a great sports enthusiast (he was Sheffield Wednesday's chairman and a big supporter of improved facilities for young people) and so would have been consoled that the site was converted into a swimming complex. It has become a leading sports training centre, is home to successful volleyball teams and divers, and offers a wide range of activities for schools.

The building of the new Ponds Forge Swimming Complex, moving towards completion in 1990. The development was completed in early 1991.

Sir Charles Clegg　Joseph B Wostinholm　"Billy" Whitham　Colonel Nathaniel Creswick

Sir Charles Clegg was known in his day as "the Napoleon of Soccer" for the Sheffield solicitor was chairman of the Football Association from 1890 to 1937 and was one of the most powerful and influential figures in the game. He played in the first England-Scotland match and refereed FA Cup Finals and internationals, and, of course, he was head of the Sheffield & Hallamshire FA.

Joseph B.Wostinholm was secretary of Yorkshire CCC and of the Bramall Lane Ground Committee in those pioneering years when, even though cricket was not paying its way, the authorities resented the rise of the "new" game called football. Wostinholm was one of the people who knowing something had to be done to make the ground profitable, found ways to exploit its potential and developed its reputation as an venue for a wide range of sports.

"Billy" Whitham was the legendary cricket scorecard seller who travelled throughout Yorkshire but was based in Sheffield, where he had worked in the local trades before someone gave him a printing machine as a gift and he turned it to great profit. He later printed the first football programmes in the town.

Colonel Nathaniel Creswick was best known in the town as a military man, but his real claim to fame was as one of the founders of Sheffield FC, the world's oldest football club, in 1857. Creswick, who was a solicitor, and his friend William Prest, a local wine merchant, were said to have dreamed up the notion of forming a football club while taking a Sunday stroll ...and the club's first headquarters were a greenhouse in a field off Queen's Road!

This picture, taken in Sheffield Town Hall in November 1979, recalls the unique occasion when a civic reception planned to celebrate Seb Coe's four world records became instead a dinner attended by 250 people, including some 200 of the city's greatest living sporting heroes, past and present. The idea was put to the Lord Mayor by *Morning Telegraph* sports editor Benny Hill, who tracked down the famous and forgotten from every sporting field. Among those present were football stars Tony Currie, Gordon Banks, former England cricket captain Norman Yardley, Olympic race-walking champion John Warhurst, and Football Association chairman Sir Andrew Stephen.

Seb Coe, who collected two Olympic golds at 1,500 metres and two at 800 metres, was one of the greatest athletes produced by Sheffield, and here the former Abbeydale and Tapton schoolboy is seen training in Marlborough Road in 1979.

There were few more popular local athletes in the years between the wars than Ernest Harper, who took up distance running seriously after winning the Stannington steeplechase in 1921 and went on to become a great Sheffield hero and one of the city's most outstanding sporting ambassadors. In his time, Harper collected his share of Yorkshire, Northern, National and International titles, but, while his triumph in the world cross-country championship in Brussels in 1926 was perhaps his best achievement, he will always be remembered for his silver medal success in the 1936 Olympics in Berlin ...because he handed the gold to a young Japanese runner with a great sporting gesture. When Kitie Son, with whom he ran shoulder to shoulder for much of the race, wanted to make an early push for the front, Harper urged the lad to bide his time and not risk burning himself out. The youngster did as he was told ...and pipped his "coach" by two minutes! When Harper retired his popularity was such that a local subscription was raised to buy him a house. Later he emigrated to Australia, where he spent the last 21 years of his life.

George Littlewood (1859-1912), who lived at Darnall, was known as "the Prince of the Peds", being the man who, in 1888 at New York's Madison Square Garden, set a world record which stood for 96 years. In one of the notorious six-day "go-as-you-please" events (a mix of running and walking continuously round an indoor track) which were so popular in the Victorian era, he covered almost 624 miles. He was the only man in this sport's history to twice top 600 miles, and he was also the first "ped" to win three six-day races to claim the coveted Astley Belt – awarded by the Lincolnshire MP, Sir John Astley, who sponsored a succession of events which made pedestrianism one of the most popular and lucrative athletic activities of the period. Incidentally, a popular local venue for these gruelling six-day events was the Edmond Road Drill Hall.

Husband and wife John and Sheila Sherwood were both outstanding Sheffield athletes whose careers touched a peak of success in the 1960s. At the 1968 Mexico Olympics, John won a bronze in the hurdles while Sheila collected a silver in the long jump. John won medals in Commonwealth and European events, and Sheila was a Commonwealth gold medalist. They each received the MBE in 1975.

The identity of this rider of an old penny farthing bike is unknown, but the picture, taken in 1887, evokes a forgotten era in local sport, and it is especially interesting to note that the scene of the race in which he competed was the old Sheaf House ground which, of course, no longer exists. This famous sports venue was just up the road from Bramall Lane, and it was here that many epic athletics meetings were staged. It will also be of interest to note that the ground was often used by Sheffield Wednesday before they had their own headquarters, and, indeed, Sheffield United's first official match in the town was actually staged here in 1889 rather than down at the Lane!

THE STAR, Monday, November 17, 1947
Victory Was "Net"
Result—By Heap
THIRTY ODD THOUSAND PETRIFIED SPECTATORS SAW WEDNESDAY AND FULHAM SET OFF AT SUCH A CRACKING PACE THAT THEY WERE TEMPTED TO JOIN IN TO GET WARM
WEDNESDAYS OPENING GOAL, BY ROGERS, TORE THROUGH THE SIDE NET, AND A WEDNESDAY BACK-ROOM BOY,—A KNITTER-UP OF GOAL NETS—NIPPED SMARTLY ON TO THE JOB, AND PUT THE MATTER RIGHT
THE FULHAM BOYS SEEMED A TEENY BIT CROSS WHEN A GOAL THEY'D BANKED ON, WAS DISALLOWED
WE LIKED THE COOL WAY IN WHICH QUIGLEY PICKED HIS SPOT OF NET - TO SCORE THE SECOND
47 ACROSS, 3 DOWN
AND STILL HARPING ON NETS, ALF SAYS,—
PERHAPS THEY'LL GET SOME OLD FISHING NETS TRANSFERRED FROM GRIMSBY

When you think of sporting journalism in Sheffield down the years, the names of Fred Walters, Frank Stainton, Richard A Sparling, Monty Marston and several writers of more recent vintage will come to mind, but cartoonist Harry Heap, who worked for *The Star* from 1928 to 1965, always had a special place in the affection of readers. This 1947 cartoon, featuring the famous character, Alf, was typical of Harry's work.

Arthur Lees, once the club professional at Dore & Totley, was one of the finest golfers ever produced by Sheffield, and, after his move to Sunningdale, he enjoyed outstanding success in international tournaments and as a Ryder Cup player in the 1940s and 1950s. Incidentally, this caricature of Lees was the work of *Sheffield Telegraph* cartoonist John Harris, who later earned fame as an author whose best-selling novels included "The Sea Shall Not Have Them".

Sheffield United soccer star Jimmy Hagan was not known as a cricketer, but the idol of Bramall Lane – one of the finest players ever to wear the red-and-white – opened a sports outfitter's shop in London Road towards the end of his playing career, and here he is seen explaining the merits of a bat to a customer. Hagan was in partnership with Harold Brook, his Blades teammate.

Here's a picture which will evoke nostalgia for many old Sheffielders …a couple of lads from Darnall, George Bowers and Harry Standish, whose great passion in the 1920s was that popular old local pastime of pigeon fancying.

The Hillsborough Boys Club, housed in the former Soldiers' Home opposite the barracks in Langsett Road, was a terrific breeding ground for sportsmen, especially in that era when Capt,. Stanley Royle was the warden. This picture, taken in 1975, shows lads getting tips from Ronnie Crookes, Freddie Smith and Henry Hall – three notable old boxers. The most famous of these was Hall (right), who had some 300 bouts as an amateur before turning professional in 1945 and going on to become British welterweight champion in 1948 when he beat Ernie Roderick.

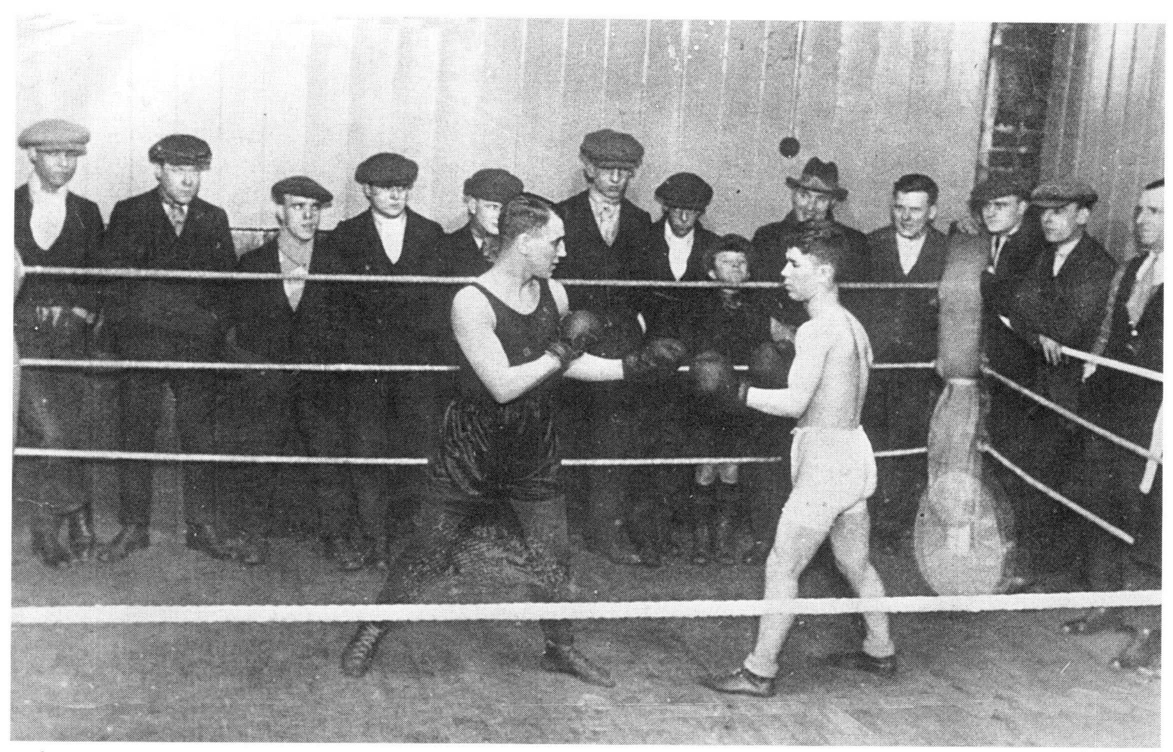

A classic picture from the late 1920s of a training session in which the legendary Sheffield boxer, Johnny Cuthbert, is watched by cloth-capped supporters as he gets in some sparring. When Cuthbert captured the British featherweight title in 1927, thousands turned out to see him arrive home with his Lonsdale Belt. He completed a double in 1932 when he lifted the British lightweight championship. Other famous Sheffield fighters down the years have included Gus Platts, Billy Calvert, Henry Hall, Bomber Graham and Johnny Nelson.

The bowling greens in Sheffield's parks have always enjoyed great popularity and the city and surrounding districts have bred many outstanding players. This picture was probably taken when the new pavilion was opened on the Ecclesfield Park green in the 1950s, for local industrial leader, Sir Harold West (right), is sharing a joke with George Shaw, who was secretary of the veterans' club and did much to promote the cause among his age group in the village.

This is a long-lost picture of the Sheffield Boys team which brought the English Schools Trophy to the city for the fifth time in June 1925 when they visited Brighton Boys in the Final and won 1-0 with a goal from outside-left Bert Palfreyman – who thus emulated his hero, Freddie Tunstall, who had scored Sheffield United's winner in the 1925 FA Cup Final at Wembley a few weeks earlier.
The great hero of the team was Newhall's Harry Gooney (he's the one with the ball on the front row). Not only captain of his school and the city teams, he was the first local lad to skipper England Boys. After turning professional, he enjoyed only a modest career with Sheffield United, Plymouth and Luton. He later worked for the Yorkshire Electricity Board.

The lad to look for in this 1942-43 Owler Lane School team is a certain Derek Dooley, who, though at the time one of the smallest players in the side, went on to become a giant centre-forward and a prolific marksman in a Sheffield Wednesday career brought to an abrupt and tragic halt when he had to have his leg amputated in February 1953. Dooley was later Wednesday's manager and completed a notable double in a remarkable career in local football when he became a director, then managing director, of Sheffield United.

After his playing career had been prematurely ended, Derek Dooley remained a folklore figure in local football, and appeared on *This is Your Life* when it was compared by Eamonn Andrews. This studio picture shows Derek, wife Sylvia and son Martyn with family and friends after the "live" screening.

The Star Walk, which was launched in 1922 and was from the outset a race for novices which was traditionally staged on Whit Tuesday, quickly regained its pre-war popularity with competitors and public when it was resumed in 1945. Here great crowds (requiring the attendance of a mounted policeman) watch the start of the 1947 event. Note that staff at Cole Brothers' store are viewing from the windows.

GARAGE
LYONS' TEA COFFEE AND COCOA
64
Ty-phoo
Dr J. COLLIS BROWNES CHLORODYNE
BOVRIL

Opposite page: This shot of Jack Woods winning the 1938 Star Walk is of special interest because it is probably the only surviving photograph which shows the buildings which stood opposite the old Corporation Street baths, on that plot of land between the bottom of Pitsmoor Road and Chatham Street. In modern times the site is occupied by a petrol station. (Incidentally, this picture has a special place in Star Walk history, for Jack Woods, then 17, was the third of a trio of brothers who won the event between 1935 and 1938 – a unique achievement.)

Bill Woodward, from Pitsmoor, was involved in one of the most dramatic finishes in the history of The Star Walk when he raced to victory in record time on the 30th anniversary of the event in 1952. Woodward and his wife, Brenda, later emigrated to Australia.

This picture, taken at the old Sheffield Corporation Transport Ground at Meadowhead in 1952, evokes memories of a time when there seemed to be a major sports day being staged on at least one of the many local arenas every Saturday in the summer. Here Dick Holland wins a seven-mile walk, and the youngster who was about to greet him as he broke the tape is seen dashing clear because *The Star's* photographer, Frank Travers, politely told him to "Shift!"

Another event which enjoyed immense popularity in the immediate post-war era was the *Sheffield Telegraph* marathon, which started in Doncaster and finished in Furnival Road, near the Sheffield Victoria railway station. It was usually run at Easter, and this shot of the finish of the 1946 event illustrates how the holiday crowds thronged to witness the action.

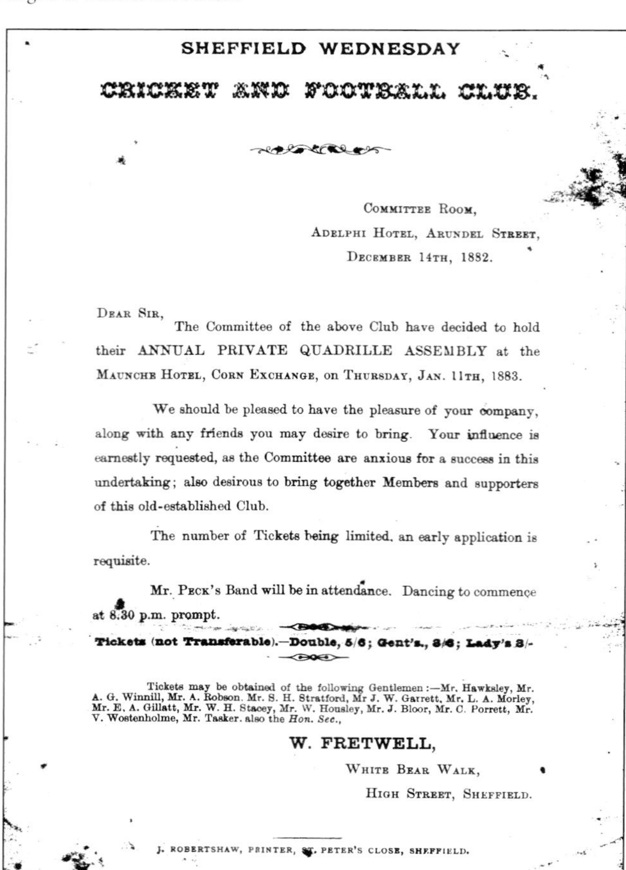

SHEFFIELD WEDNESDAY

CRICKET AND FOOTBALL CLUB.

COMMITTEE ROOM,
ADELPHI HOTEL, ARUNDEL STREET,
DECEMBER 14TH, 1882.

DEAR SIR,
The Committee of the above Club have decided to hold their ANNUAL PRIVATE QUADRILLE ASSEMBLY at the MAUNCHE HOTEL, CORN EXCHANGE, on THURSDAY, JAN. 11TH, 1883.

We should be pleased to have the pleasure of your company, along with any friends you may desire to bring. Your influence is earnestly requested, as the Committee are anxious for a success in this undertaking; also desirous to bring together Members and supporters of this old-established Club.

The number of Tickets being limited, an early application is requisite.

Mr. PECK's Band will be in attendance. Dancing to commence at 8.30 p.m. prompt.

Tickets (not Transferable).—Double, 5/6; Gent's., 3/6; Lady's 3/-

Tickets may be obtained of the following Gentlemen:—Mr. Hawksley, Mr. A. G. Winnill, Mr. A. Robson. Mr. S. H. Stratford, Mr J. W. Garrett, Mr. L. A. Morley, Mr. E. A. Gillatt, Mr. W. H. Stacey, Mr. W. Housley, Mr. J. Bloor, Mr. C. Porrett, Mr. V. Wostenholme, Mr. Tasker. also the *Hon. Sec.*,

W. FRETWELL,
WHITE BEAR WALK,
HIGH STREET, SHEFFIELD.

J. ROBERTSHAW, PRINTER, ST. PETER'S CLOSE, SHEFFIELD.

An intriguing glimpse into the social life of members of the Sheffield Wednesday Cricket and Football club less than a year before the two sections chose to go their separate ways. It was the first formal dinner held by the club.

The Adelphi Hotel (Arundel Street), which stood where the Crucible Theatre is now, was kept by Harry Sampson, a famous single-wicket cricketer in the Victorian era, and here, in one of those upper rooms, local sportsmen met to arrange the creation of the Sheffield United Cricket Club and the building of Bramall Lane (1854), and to form the Yorkshire CCC (1863) and the Sheffield Wednesday Football Club (1867).

The Earl of Arundel & Surrey (Queen's Road) was where Sheffield Wednesday had their first changing rooms after they turned professional in 1887. Initially, after spending £5,000 on converting their new Olive Grove ground from a swampy field into a decent football pitch and enclosure, the club could not afford to complete dressing rooms. So, for the first few months, the players had to use facilities offered by the local pub, and, though it meant they had to walk across a road and over a railway bridge to reach the ground (and definitely could not escape irate supporters!) they didn't mind too much.

The Bull & Mouth (Waingate) has a special place in Wednesday's history because it was in this pub in the spring of 1891 that the club recruited one of its greatest players, a winger called Fred Spiksley, who was destined to become the darling of Olive Grove and an England international. Spiksley, who hailed from Gainsborough, had been to Accrington and agreed to sign for them, but, on his way home to Lincolnshire, he was stranded in Sheffield. He had to stay overnight in the town, and, in the Bull & Mouth, bumped into a Wednesday player called Fred Thompson, who urged him to delay signing for Accrington until he had spoken to Wednesday's president, John Holmes. Holmes got his man by offering him an extra ten shillings (50p) a week plus a job in the composing room of the *Sheffield Telegraph*.

Sporting heroes set the fashion in long hair ...Sheffield United's Tony Currie (left) and Wednesday's Ken Knighton snapped at a Town Hall reception in the 1970s. Currie was one of the many bargain signings made by the late John Harris, arriving from Watford in 1968, and going on to make over 300 appearances in which he emerged as United's greatest idol since Jimmy Hagan. Knighton had already served five clubs before he joined Wednesday in 1973, and he is best remembered for the goal with which he saved the Owls from relegation in 1974.

The bare cheek of it ...the day in 1974 when the Sheffield Wednesday-York City match at Hillsborough was interrupted by the arrival on the pitch of an elderly streaker.

Shiregreen CC, one of the top League cricket clubs in Sheffield, enjoyed a vintage summer in 1948 when they captured the Yorkshire Council Championship under the captaincy of Jackie Thomson and with a side that included the likes of Doug Smith, Harold Pears and Ronnie Rodgers. Incidentally, the latter's name will be familiar to many as that of a man who gave outstanding service to local football, for Ronnie was the dedicated secretary of Norton Woodseats FC over a very long period.

Sheffield Collegiate is one of the famous names of local cricket, and their Abbeydale Park ground has been the South Yorkshire base for Yorkshire matches since 1974. This picture is of a Collegiate side from the late 1890s. Back row (left to right): Pring, Frank Atkin, George Bott, F.Wood, Revd A.Wilson. Middle row: J.W.Aizlewood, J.M.Clayton, H.B.Willey, C.R.Wilson, Dr H.Lockwood. Front: H.Willey, E.R.Wilson.

Sheffield's first major cricket ground, built at Darnall in the early 1820s. In its time it was a popular venue which had a national reputation, but, later, Hyde Park enjoyed some success. However, the real turning point for cricket in the town was the building of Bramall Lane in the mid-1850s.

Scorebox view to the Bawtry Road ground where Sheffield United Cricket Club eventually settled after being forced to leave Bramall Lane in 1973. For a time they played at Dore, and there was at one stage a suggestion of an amalgamation with Sheffield Collegiate, but finding the old Firth Vickers ground gave the club a new lease of life.

This line drawing, which used to be featured on the front of Sheffield United's match programme some 40 or more years ago, gives a fair impression of what the Bramall Lane ground looked like when it was still a home of cricket as well as football.

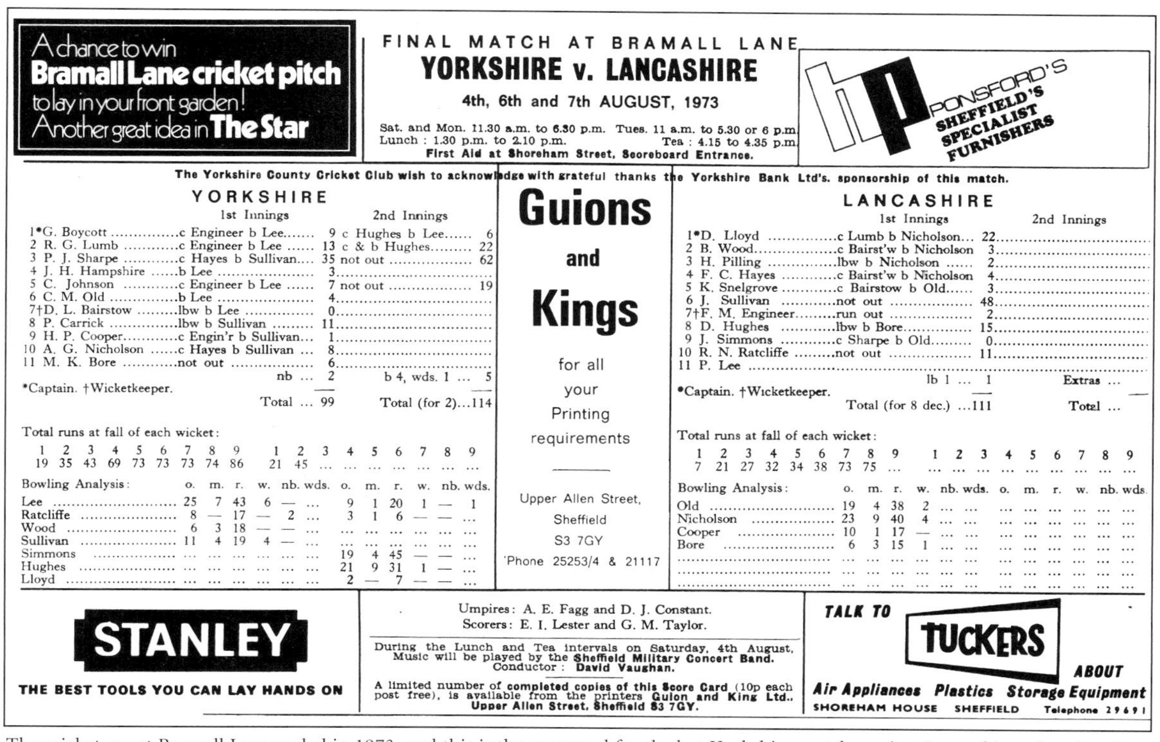

A chance to win Bramall Lane cricket pitch to lay in your front garden! Another great idea in The Star

FINAL MATCH AT BRAMALL LANE

YORKSHIRE v. LANCASHIRE

4th, 6th and 7th AUGUST, 1973

Sat. and Mon. 11.30 a.m. to 6.30 p.m. Tues. 11 a.m. to 5.30 or 6 p.m.
Lunch : 1.30 p.m. to 2.10 p.m. Tea : 4.15 to 4.35 p.m.
First Aid at Shoreham Street, Scoreboard Entrance.

hp PONSFORD'S SHEFFIELD'S SPECIALIST FURNISHERS

The Yorkshire County Cricket Club wish to acknowledge with grateful thanks the Yorkshire Bank Ltd's. sponsorship of this match.

YORKSHIRE

	1st Innings		2nd Innings	
1*G. Boycott	c Engineer b Lee	9	c Hughes b Lee	6
2 R. G. Lumb	c Engineer b Lee	13	c & b Hughes	22
3 P. J. Sharpe	c Hayes b Sullivan	35	not out	62
4 J. H. Hampshire	b Lee	3		
5 C. Johnson	c Engineer b Lee	7	not out	19
6 C. M. Old	b Lee	4		
7†D. L. Bairstow	lbw b Lee	0		
8 P. Carrick	lbw b Sullivan	11		
9 H. P. Cooper	c Engin'r b Sullivan	1		
10 A. G. Nicholson	c Hayes b Sullivan	8		
11 M. K. Bore	not out	6		
	nb	2	b 4, wds. 1	5
	Total	99	Total (for 2)	114

*Captain. †Wicketkeeper.

Total runs at fall of each wicket:

	1	2	3	4	5	6	7	8	9
1st Innings	19	35	43	69	73	73	73	74	86
2nd Innings	21	45	...	...	...	...	...	...	...

Bowling Analysis	o.	m.	r.	w.	nb.	wds.	o.	m.	r.	w.	nb.	wds.
Lee	25	7	43	6	—	...	9	1	20	1	—	1
Ratcliffe	8	—	17	—	2	...	3	1	6	—	—	...
Wood	6	3	18	—	—	...	...	...	...	...	...	...
Sullivan	11	4	19	4	—	...	...	...	...	...	...	...
Simmons	...	...	...	...	...	...	19	4	45	—	—	...
Hughes	...	...	...	...	...	...	21	9	31	1	—	...
Lloyd	...	...	...	...	...	...	2	—	7	—	—	...

Guions and Kings for all your Printing requirements

Upper Allen Street, Sheffield S3 7GY
'Phone 25253/4 & 21117

LANCASHIRE

	1st Innings		2nd Innings	
1*D. Lloyd	c Lumb b Nicholson	22		
2 B. Wood	c Bairst'w b Nicholson	3		
3 H. Pilling	lbw b Nicholson	2		
4 F. C. Hayes	c Bairst'w b Nicholson	4		
5 K. Snelgrove	c Bairstow b Old	3		
6 J. Sullivan	not out	48		
7†F. M. Engineer	run out	2		
8 D. Hughes	lbw b Bore	15		
9 J. Simmons	c Sharpe b Old	0		
10 R. N. Ratcliffe	not out	11		
11 P. Lee				
	lb 1	1	Extras	...
	Total (for 8 dec.)	111	Total	...

*Captain. †Wicketkeeper.

Total runs at fall of each wicket:

	1	2	3	4	5	6	7	8	9
1st Innings	7	21	27	32	34	38	73	75	...
2nd Innings	...	...	...	...	...	...	...	...	...

Bowling Analysis	o.	m.	r.	w.	nb.	wds.	o.	m.	r.	w.	nb.	wds.
Old	19	4	38	2	...	...	...	...	...	...	...	...
Nicholson	23	9	40	4	...	...	...	...	...	...	...	...
Cooper	10	1	17	—	...	...	...	...	...	...	...	...
Bore	6	3	15	1	...	...	...	...	...	...	...	...

STANLEY
THE BEST TOOLS YOU CAN LAY HANDS ON

Umpires: A. E. Fagg and D. J. Constant.
Scorers: E. I. Lester and G. M. Taylor.

During the Lunch and Tea intervals on Saturday, 4th August, Music will be played by the Sheffield Military Concert Band. Conductor: David Vaughan.

A limited number of completed copies of this Score Card (10p each post free), is available from the printers Guion and King Ltd., Upper Allen Street, Sheffield S3 7GY.

TALK TO TUCKERS ABOUT
Air Appliances Plastics Storage Equipment
SHOREHAM HOUSE SHEFFIELD Telephone 29691

The cricket era at Bramall Lane ended in 1973, and this is the scorecard for the last Yorkshire match, against Lancashire, played at the ground. Sadly, the rain made the finale something of an anticlimax.

By mid-August 1973 the famous turf on the cricket side at Bramall Lane was being cut up, ready for sale to enthusiasts who wanted something by which to remember an era which had come to an end after 118 years.

The new South Stand, built right across the area where so many of Yorkshire cricket's all-time greats had trodden the hallowed turf, was opened in August 1975, but for some time afterwards the old pavilion remained until it was finally demolished in the late 1970s.

This picture, which shows Sheffield's Roger Taylor, a Wimbledon semi-finalist, in action, serves to remind us that, in its time, Bramall Lane has staged a remarkable range of sporting activities. It has been the venue for soccer internationals, an FA Cup Final, Rugby League, athletics, lacrosse, and, of course, a cricket Test.

This action shot from a United game in the 1920s is of special interest in that it shows the old John Street stand packed to capacity and features the old rooftop Press Box ...an ideal location in the distant days when reporters used to send their messages back to the office by pigeon! In later years the Pressmen were housed in the back of the stand and the old box disappeared ...though many newspapermen will still remember some part of it survived and was used as a half-time refreshment room.

A more recent view of Bramall Lane which is of interest because it shows the Shoreham Street end before its conversion to a seating area, and, of course, the John Street stand on the far side was demolished in the summer of 1994 to remove a famous landmark and transform the look of the ground.

Entertainment in Sheffield

Tommy Youdan and The Surrey Music Hall

Tommy Youdan holds a special place in local theatrical folklore: billed as Sheffield's first great showman and the man who created two of the most famous houses of entertainment in the town.

Our picture of the old Surrey Music Hall on West Bar recalls that this popular venue of 130 years ago went the way of so many Sheffield theatres – destroyed by an epic fire. Youdan, however, recovered from this setback and went on to create the Alexandra Theatre, the famous "Old Alex:, a site subsequently cleared to make way for the opening up of Castlegate in November 1930.

Remarkably, Youdan, who came from near Doncaster, began his working life as an agricultural labourer, but, with a head filled with romantic notions, he always said he arrived in Sheffield as a teenager expecting to find the streets paved with gold, went into silver (in James Dixon's Cornish Works), and threw the job up to take a beerhouse in the Park district. Later he took a public house in West Bar called Spink's Nest – and converted it into a music hall.

He managed to achieve this by gradually buying up the adjoining properties and knocking them into a unique night spot which incorporated a concert room, a ballroom and a restaurant ... plus an underground museum and, at one stage, a menagerie with animals from Wingerworth Hall.

Youdan, the great publicist, used every trick he knew to keep his theatre in the news, but the news the Music Hall made on 25 March 1865 was far from welcome. Called from his bed at soon after 2 am, he reached West Bar to find the empty theatre engulfed in flames ...and, as he admitted later, he wept like a child. But nobody was surprised when, within six months, Youdan was back in business, converting a former storeroom into the Alexandra, where he spent the last nine years of his career. He died in September 1876.

Jewell and Warriss

Sheffield cousins Jimmy Jewell and Ben Warriss (Jimmy is on the left) are still remembered as the best comedy team the city has ever produced.

The pair, whose mothers were sisters, were born within six months of each other in 1909 – in the same bed and the same Andover Street, Pitsmoor, house.

In fact, they grew up in Cobden View Road, Crookes, and, though it was evident that both were destined for a career in show business, they did not become a duo until they were 25 years old …and it happened by accident.

Ben once said: "We were both on the same bill as solo acts at Newcastle when it emerged that a double act had failed to turn up. We kidded the manager that we had appeared as a duo many times (even though we hadn't) and could fill in without rehearsal.

"After we'd gone on and been a hit, someone said we should develop the act. We did and it wasn't long before we were topping the bill in variety theatres throughout the country."

However, they touched a peak of popularity in the early post-war years, when, in the pre-TV era, they had a smash-hit radio series. *Up The Pole*, topped the bill at the London Palladium and appeared on the *Ed Sullivan Show* on American TV – the most coveted prize in show business at that time. At their peak they were earning £1,000 a week when that was really big money.

Ben once admitted that he and Jimmy were as different as chalk and cheese in terms of personality. Jimmy, the clown, just happened to be the partner who was serious, methodical and a worrier off stage; Ben was the easy-going lad, a bit of playboy, who preferred to live for the moment and enjoy life. But they were ideal partners, and driven by a fierce family loyalty.

When they ended their formal partnership in 1967, Jimmy was the first to go into the legitimate theatre, and he made a big success of "going straight" on television. Ben was to follow suit.

Ben recalled that when they were boys they were always fighting, so much so that the headmaster at Broomhill School refused to have them both. Ben stayed, Jimmy went to another school.

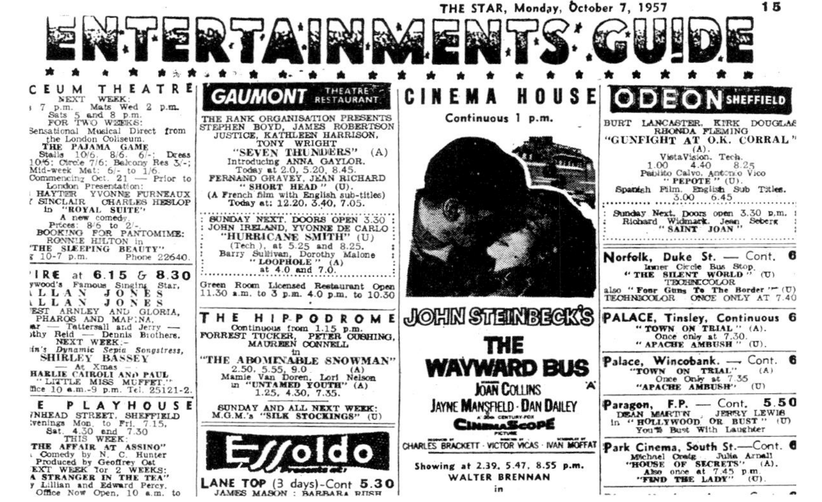

THE STAR, Monday, October 7, 1957 15

ENTERTAINMENTS GUIDE

CEUM THEATRE
NEXT WEEK:
7 p.m. Mats Wed 2 p.m.
Sats 5 and 8 p.m.
FOR TWO WEEKS:
Sensational Musical Direct from the London Coliseum.
THE PAJAMA GAME
Stalls 10/6, 8/6, 6/-; Dress 10/6; Circle 7/6; Balcony Res 3/-; Mid-week Mat: 6/- to 1/6.
Commencing Oct. 21 — Prior to London Presentation:
HAYTER YVONNE FURNEAUX
SINCLAIR CHARLES HESLOP
in "ROYAL SUITE"
A new comedy.
Prices: 8/6 to 2/-.
BOOKING FOR PANTOMIME:
RONNIE HILTON in
"THE SLEEPING BEAUTY"
10-7 p.m. Phone 22640.

IRE at 6.15 & 8.30
ywood's Famous Singing Star,
LLAN JONES
LLAN JONES
EST ARNLEY AND GLORIA,
PHAROS AND MARINA,
ar — Tattersall and Jerry —
thy Reid — Dennis Brothers.
NEXT WEEK:-
in's *Dynamic Sepia Songstress,*
SHIRLEY BASSEY
— At Xmas —
HARLIE CAIROLI AND PAUL
"LITTLE MISS MUFFET."
ffice 10 a.m.-9 p.m. Tel. 25121-2.

E PLAYHOUSE
NHEAD STREET, SHEFFIELD
venings Mon. to Fri. 7.15,
Sat. 4.30 and 7.30
THIS WEEK:
THE AFFAIR AT ASSINO"
Comedy by N. C. Hunter
Produced by Geoffrey Ost
EXT WEEK for 2 WEEKS:
A STRANGER IN THE TEA"
y Lillian and Edward Percy.
Office Now Open, 10 a.m. to

GAUMONT THEATRE RESTAURANT
THE RANK ORGANISATION PRESENTS
STEPHEN BOYD, JAMES ROBERTSON JUSTICE, KATHLEEN HARRISON, TONY WRIGHT
"SEVEN THUNDERS" (A)
Introducing ANNA GAYLOR.
Today at 2.0, 5.20, 8.45.
FERNAND GRAVEY, JEAN RICHARD
"SHORT HEAD" (U).
(A French film with English sub-titles)
Today at: 12.20, 3.40, 7.05.
SUNDAY NEXT. DOORS OPEN 3.30
JOHN IRELAND, YVONNE DE CARLO
"HURRICANE SMITH" (U)
(Tech.), at 5.25 and 8.25.
Barry Sullivan, Dorothy Malone
"LOOPHOLE" (A)
at 4.0 and 7.0.
Green Room Licensed Restaurant Open 11.30 a.m. to 3 p.m. 4.0 p.m. to 10.30

THE HIPPODROME
Continuous from 1.15 p.m.
FORREST TUCKER, PETER CUSHING, MAUREEN CONNELL
in
"THE ABOMINABLE SNOWMAN"
2.50, 5.55, 9.0 (A)
Mamie Van Doren, Lori Nelson
in "UNTAMED YOUTH" (A)
1.25, 4.30, 7.35.
SUNDAY AND ALL NEXT WEEK:
M.G.M.'s "SILK STOCKINGS" (U)

Essoldo
LANE TOP (3 days)-Cont 5.30
JAMES MASON : BARBARA RUSH

CINEMA HOUSE
Continuous 1 p.m.
JOHN STEINBECK'S
THE WAYWARD BUS 'A'
JOAN COLLINS
JAYNE MANSFIELD · DAN DAILEY
CINEMASCOPE
CHARLES BRACKETT · VICTOR VICAS · IVAN MOFFAT
Showing at 2.39, 5.47, 8.55 p.m.
WALTER BRENNAN
in

ODEON SHEFFIELD
BURT LANCASTER, KIRK DOUGLAS
RHONDA FLEMING
"GUNFIGHT AT O.K. CORRAL"
(A).
VistaVision. Tech.
1.00 4.40 8.25
Pablito Calvo, Antonio Vico
"PEPOTE" (U).
Spanish Film. English Sub Titles.
3.00 6.45
Sunday Next. Doors open 3.30 p.m.
Richard Widmark. Jean Seberg
"SAINT JOAN"

Norfolk, Duke St. — Cont. 6
Inner Circle Bus Stop.
"THE SILENT WORLD" (U)
TECHNICOLOR
also "Four Guns To The Border" (U)
TECHNICOLOR ONCE ONLY AT 7.40

PALACE, Tinsley, Continuous 6
"TOWN ON TRIAL" (A).
Once only at 7.30.
"APACHE AMBUSH" (U).

Palace, Wincobank. — Cont. 6
"TOWN ON TRIAL" (A)
Once Only at 7.35
"APACHE AMBUSH" (U)

Paragon, F.P. — Cont. 5.50
DEAN MARTIN JERRY LEWIS
in "HOLLYWOOD OR BUST" (U)
You'll Bust With Laughter

Park Cinema, South St.—Cont. 6
Michael Craig Julia Arnall
"HOUSE OF SECRETS" (A).
Also once at 7.45 p.m.
"FIND THE LADY" (U).

A reproduction of the Entertainments Guide from *The Star*, dated Monday, 7 October 1957, just to remind us of some of the once familiar cinemas and theatres where we enjoyed so many good times.

Ecclesfield Silver Prize Band on parade.

The bandstand in Weston Park is the centre of attention.

This picture of the Worrall Male Voice Choir performing with the James Shepherd Versatile Brass at the Lyceum Theatre in March 1992 (it was a fund raising concert for Weston Park Hospital) serves to remind us how popular choirs and brass bands are in the Sheffield region.

The Mayor and his family with Corporation officials at a Civic social gathering in 1887, possibly a function connected with celebrating Queen Victoria's Jubilee.

Patrons of the Milton Arms in Thomas Street face the camera while awaiting transport to take them for a day out – at the seaside, or, it has been suggested, at the races at Doncaster.

Members of Mosborough Druids Club, pictured with banner in front of the Blue Bell, ahead of their annual parade.

Oughtibridge Church Walk, circa 1960.

Arnold Hemingfield, of Shiregreen, prepares to take an Ecclesfield party on an outing, possibly around 1913.

Schooldays in Sheffield

This group of infants were captured on one of the first school photographs organised at the Huntsman's Gardens School around 1906.

A later group of boys at Huntsman's Gardens, around 1922.

Boys at Tinsley School, probably in the early 1930s.

There was a time in that part of Sheffield's old East End which was long since demolished when the name Joe Middleton was synonymous with entertainment, even though his full-time job was as a first-hand melter at the River Don Works of the English Steel Corporation. Joe, who followed in his father's footsteps as a coster comedian, gained his early experience by organising concerts for the unemployed (as in this picture) in the backyards in and around the family home in Newark Street, which was just off Attercliffe Common before the district disappeared in the cause of redevelopment. Joe, who used to sing in the style of the legendary G.H.Elliott ("The Chocolate Coloured Coon") later graduated to the local Adelphi Cinema and the famous old Attercliffe Palace, and then to starring roles at the Empire and the new City Hall. Subsequently, with partners Frank Jackman and Charlie Burrell, he topped the bills all over Yorkshire and Lancashire before spending his last years on the Sheffield club circuit.

May Day concert at Firshill Infants School, 1934.

Unfortunately, it has proved impossible to put a date or place on this picture of Sheffield youngsters enjoying a street party, but it seems likely to have been a royal occasion, perhaps the 1937 Coronation.

Children at Newhall School in the late 1940s.

"Dressing Up" was once part of the curriculum at some schools, much of the delight of infants like these children acting out their parts in the yard at Swallownest School.

Woodhouse Grammar School's hockey team 1959-60.

Postscript

This postcard, depicting a Sheffield evening full of gloom, smoke and puthering chimneys, was once the traditional image of a city famed for its steel and cutlery. But things have changed and a new, brighter Sheffield had been in existence long before circumstances induced a decline in local traditional industries. An interesting fact is that in 1993 Sheffield produced as much steel as it did in 1942. It is not a city without its problems – like learning to cope with all the inconvenience caused while Supertram is being established – but it's home and we love it ...and, as the sales of the original *Images of Sheffield* in "foreign" parts showed, there's many, many exiles who still remember it with great affection.

We hope, whether you're at home or away, you've enjoyed this second dose of Images. Sheffield isn't like this postcard... Nowt like it!